The Bible of Dark Psychology

The Only Book You'll Ever Need to Understand People's Thoughts, Actions, and How to Change Them.

HALBERT WARD

TABLE OF CONTENTS

INTRODUCTION

Do you ever wonder how to get your way with colleagues, bosses, and others? Would you like to learn how to spot and use the tactics of dark psychology to your advantage? If yes, read on because this book will show you how to do these things. If you're tired of being manipulated, this book is for you. If you want to learn how to "manipulate" others, this book is also for you.

Learning to persuade or manipulate others for good reasons isn't necessarily bad. You can use these skills to encourage your child to eat, convince a friend to see a therapist, negotiate deals, or motivate your team at work. The power of influence is a tool; like any tool, its impact depends on how you wield it.

Remember when you found yourself signing up for a gym membership you didn't want? Your friend insisted it was for your good, and before you knew it, you were committed. Or there was a day you reluctantly agreed to meet a friend's charming coworker despite telling them repeatedly you weren't ready for a new relationship. Interestingly enough, that coworker turned out to be your soulmate. These moments are not just coincidences but instances where subtle manipulation plays a role in steering your decisions.

These scenarios highlight a common thread in our lives: manipulation. It's everywhere, and often, we don't even realize it's happening. Manipulation is a fact of life, and it's inevitable. While some people manipulate for the target's benefit, others do it for their own gain. Some enjoy deceiving and controlling those they see as vulnerable.

In a world full of such individuals, it's crucial to arm yourself with the knowledge of dark psychology. It's easy to trust that people want the best for you, but some are only interested in their needs and will exploit you without a second thought. Understanding these tactics is not just about self-defense; it's about being proactive and taking control of your interactions and outcomes.

Energy vampires and predators are everywhere, using dark psychology to deceive and control. To protect yourself, you need to understand their tactics and, if necessary, use them to your advantage. This knowledge will help you read people's thoughts, influence their actions, and change their minds. More importantly, you'll recognize when someone is trying to manipulate you, which can improve both your relationships and career. Imagine seeing through the facades and understanding the true motives behind people's actions.

Dark psychology involves using tactics of manipulation, persuasion, motivation, and coercion to achieve your desires. Depending on the individual, these tactics can be used for good or bad. People use psychological manipulation for various reasons. Nonprofits and charities use it for good, changing perspectives and making positive impacts. Managers use it to influence their workers. Corporations, politicians, and public speakers all use dark psychology techniques to get what they want. Imagine knowing how to influence people around you. This book will equip you with this knowledge and simultaneously help you identify negative manipulators in your life.

Manipulation often carries a negative connotation because no one likes being controlled. Yet, many people and companies use manipulation daily to influence lives. If you struggle to get people to do things for you, this book will teach you effective psychological manipulation techniques. We'll also explore the principles of persuasion and reveal how marketers, salespeople, and con artists manipulate others. Understanding these tactics will help unleash your persuasive powers.

Emotional intelligence is essential for personal and professional success. This book will help you understand your emotions and those of others, enhancing your ability to persuade positively and motivate yourself and others. You'll learn how to use emotional intelligence skills effectively in your interactions. They will help you gain clearer thinking and a better mindset, leading to greater achievement of your goals. We will also cover how to understand body language and use it for covert manipulation in various situations.

Manipulation isn't always negative; it can create positive changes in your life and others. Dark psychology, persuasion, and manipulation are integral to the business world and can help you in personal relationships, job searches, and achieving your goals.

I'd like to share a story that perfectly captures the power of dark psychology. A few years ago, a friend named Mary was struggling at work. Her colleague, Dan, was always one step ahead, snagging the best projects and getting the promotions. Frustrated, Mary observed Dan closely, and what she discovered changed everything.

Dan wasn't just hardworking; he was a master of subtle manipulation. He knew how to read the room, say the right things at the right time, and make people feel valued and understood. Inspired, Mary decided to learn these skills herself. She started small, using her newfound knowledge to build better relationships with her coworkers and boss. Over time, Mary's efforts paid off. She was no longer overlooked or undervalued. Instead, she became a respected and influential member of her team. Her career soared, and she achieved goals she once thought were out of reach.

This transformation wasn't about deceit or malice; it was about understanding human behavior and using that understanding to create positive outcomes. By mastering these basic psychology techniques, Mary turned her professional life around. And you can, too.

Whether you want to protect yourself from negative influences or learn to influence others without their conscious awareness, the knowledge in this book will be your key to success.

So, let’s get into it.

CHAPTER ONE:
Introduction To Dark Psychology

Do you remember walking into a store for window shopping only to leave with a bag full of clothes? Or that time your boss convinced you that staying late is your way of helping the company grow? What about that sweet talker at work who always knows what to say to get you to do something for them? We've all been there.

What do your boss, colleague, and the salesperson at the store all have in common? They know how to read people's thoughts and actions and change them. Everyone has the inherent capability to manipulate others. While many control and restrain this tendency, some don't and act on their impulses. These people often become masters of dark psychology tactics.

Dark psychology involves discovering and exploiting human weaknesses. It is the knowledge and study of the darker aspects of human behavior. It focuses on how people can exploit psychological vulnerabilities to manipulate, control, and deceive others for personal gain. It reveals much about human nature and how to use these techniques to achieve your goals.

People who have mastered the art understand how others think and feel and can manipulate them to do what they want. They know how to use coercion, deception, persuasion, and other strategies to influence emotions, thoughts, and behaviors without awareness or consent. Depending on the kind of person you are, you can either use dark psychology for good or evil. These techniques are often linked to criminal activities like scams, fraud, terrorism, and abuse. Still, they are also present in everyday situations like work, relationships, and politics. When someone masters dark psychology, it can be an incredibly powerful tool.

The concept of dark psychology has existed since ancient times, when people used superstition, suggestion, and hypnosis to control others. For instance, ancient civilizations like the Egyptians and Greeks used rituals and oracles to influence people's beliefs and actions. In medieval Europe, witchcraft and the fear of the supernatural were powerful tools for manipulation. The fear of witch hunts and accusations could control entire communities.

In the 20th century, more sophisticated techniques emerged from psychological studies. The work of Sigmund Freud and later his nephew, Edward Bernays, laid the groundwork for understanding the unconscious mind's role in influencing behavior. Bernays, often called the father of public relations, used Freud's theories to develop techniques for mass manipulation, which he applied in advertising and political propaganda. His campaigns demonstrated how powerful subconscious desires and fears could be exploited to shape public opinion and consumer behavior.

Today, dark psychology is more prevalent due to propaganda, advertising, and social media. Individuals, organizations, and groups use tactics ranging from subtle manipulation to overt coercion to achieve their goals. The digital age has amplified the reach and effectiveness of these tactics. Social media platforms, for example, are designed to exploit psychological vulnerabilities, using algorithms to keep users engaged and influence their behavior without their conscious awareness. This environment creates fertile ground for dark psychology techniques to thrive.

Dark psychology can be both fascinating and frightening. It shines a light on the darker aspects of human nature and how easily people can be influenced and manipulated without their knowledge. The more you understand about dark psychology, the better you can protect yourself from being exploited and, if necessary, use these techniques to your advantage in a responsible manner.

One of the critical aspects of dark psychology is recognizing its presence in everyday life. From marketing tactics that convince us to buy things we don't need to political campaigns that sway public opinion, dark psychology surrounds us. Understanding how these techniques work can help you become more critical and discerning in daily interactions.

As previously mentioned, people use these techniques for various reasons. Some aim for nefarious ends, while others use them beneficially. Therapists, for example, may use elements of dark psychology to help patients confront and overcome deep-seated fears and anxieties. Similarly, law enforcement professionals might use these techniques to gather crucial information from suspects or witnesses. When used for the wrong reasons, dark psychology can be harmful and result in serious consequences for both the manipulator and the victim.

The more we dive into the various dark psychology techniques, the more we will learn how they can be identified and countered. This knowledge is empowering because it enables you to recognize when someone is trying to control you or attempt to manipulate you so that you can respond appropriately.

People in authority often manipulate those around them using dark psychology. For example, a politician might use these techniques to influence the media to present a positive image, or a salesperson might convince you to buy products you don't need. Your boss could control employees with psychological tricks. Remember, these tactics could be used on anyone.

In society and pop culture, dark psychology techniques manipulate media coverage, influence public opinion, and shape political outcomes. Misinformation, fake news, and propaganda manipulate attitudes and beliefs, leading to conflict, division, and polarization. These tactics can erode democratic values and undermine trust in institutions.

Examples of dark psychology include spreading fake news during elections and using psychological techniques in marketing and advertising. While often considered unethical, some professions use these tactics advantageously. Law enforcement, for instance, gathers criminal information through dark psychology, which helps study the human mind and overcome challenges. The point is that understanding dark psychology can be beneficial. Once you grasp how it works, you can use it correctly in situations that require these strategies.

Dark psychology uses principles of basic human psychology to benefit the manipulator at the expense of others. It often involves restricting the freedom of the individual on the receiving end. But even though dark psychology tactics can influence others' thoughts, they don't work on everyone and aren't a form of sorcery. They operate within the boundaries of logic.

Practitioners use dark psychology to influence ideas without using force or traditional persuasive methods, often through techniques like operant conditioning. This technique hacks into someone's psyche, changing their behavior using external triggers. For instance, mental conditioning and repetition can be used to alter the information processing mechanisms of a vulnerable person, making them susceptible to future manipulation.

I have had people ask me how dark psychology techniques differ from normal human psychology principles. Well, the key difference lies in how they are utilized. An analogy I like using to explain this difference is the kitchen knife analogy.

Think of psychology as a kitchen knife. The knife is used to create wonderful meals in a chef's hand. The chef uses their skills to prepare delightful and nourishing foods. This is normal psychology, which involves understanding human behavior to support, heal, and improve lives.

Now, imagine the same kitchen knife in the hands of someone dangerous. Rather than prepare delicious meals, this person uses the knife to threaten, intimidate, or inflict harm. This is dark psychology. It's the same tool – understanding of human behavior – but in the wrong person's hands; it is used to manipulate, brainwash, control, and take advantage of others for personal gain.

Therefore, the difference between psychology and dark psychology is akin to that between a chef and a criminal with a kitchen knife. They both know this tool but have different intentions and outcomes. The field of psychology itself uses the knowledge of human behavior to help and heal. In contrast, dark psychology practitioners seek to exploit and harm others with that knowledge.

Unlike traditional psychology, the core concepts of dark psychology include:

- exploiting human vulnerabilities, including biases and distortions in cognition and emotion.
- influencing the subconscious mind, which makes the target unaware of what's happening.
- crossing ethical and moral lines, often at the target's expense.

Individuals who practice dark psychology employ key techniques, such as:

- **Coercion**: This is a direct and aggressive form of manipulation. It involves using intimidation, threats, or force to make an individual compliant with one's demands.
- **Deception** involves lying or providing inaccurate information to create false impressions or beliefs. It can range from small lies to elaborate schemes.
- **Persuasion**: Convincing a person to change their mind through argument or reasoning. It can be benign or harmful, depending on the context and intent.
- **Manipulation**: Subtle, indirect tactics to influence someone's decisions or behavior. Manipulation often involves playing on emotions, such as guilt or fear.

Now, these techniques encompass varying tactics used to manipulate, coerce, persuade, or deceive others. Some of the tactics include:

- **Gaslighting**: Making someone doubt their perceptions and sanity by consistently presenting false information and denying their experiences.
- **Love Bombing**: Overwhelming someone with affection, attention, and flattery to gain control over them. This tactic is often used in abusive relationships to create dependency.
- **Fear and Guilt**: Exploiting someone's fears or sense of guilt to manipulate their actions. This is common in abusive relationships and coercive environments.
- **Operant Conditioning**: Changing someone's behavior through a system of rewards and punishments. This can condition individuals to act in specific ways without their conscious awareness.

This book will delve deeper into dark psychology and its techniques, exploring how they apply in various contexts. Furthermore, we will look at specific tactics used in dark psychology, such as gaslighting, love bombing, and the use of fear and guilt. We'll also explore how these tactics are applied in different settings, from personal relationships to workplace dynamics and political campaigns.

It's important to emphasize that these techniques are about psychological manipulation, not mind control.

Story

Here's a story about two coworkers, Alex and Sarah, to help you better understand how dark psychology tactics can be wielded to manipulate you.

Alex and Sarah were colleagues at an advertising agency. They were hired around the same time for similar roles, so they started as equals. Alex was charismatic, always smiling, and seemingly quick to help others with their workload. Sarah was hardworking and diligent, knowing how to get things done precisely. Everyone could tell she was eager to prove her worth to the team and her boss.

Alex and Sarah were on the same team, meaning they had to collaborate on projects together. At first, things started on a positive note. They would brainstorm ideas, share tasks, and bond over donuts in the break room. Alex always complimented Sarah, especially regarding her attention to detail. He would say things like, "Wow, you really have a great eye for this stuff. I swear I trust your judgment more than anyone else's on our projects." Naturally, Sarah felt valued and appreciated. She loved working with Alex.

Soon, though, Sarah noticed a few changes in their interactions. She noticed Alex would ask her to write a report here and there because of "back-to-back meetings." He was always swamped. Of course, she genuinely enjoyed working with him, so she gladly took on the extra work. It didn't seem like a big deal at first – teamwork makes the dream work.

Then, there was the flattery. Alex would praise Sarah for being "incredibly efficient" in front of other coworkers and their boss, making her feel like the office MVP. "Sarah, you're a lifesaver! We couldn't do this without you," he'd say with a big grin. The praises made Sarah feel even more validated and indispensable. She was driven to keep excelling and proving herself to everyone.

As time passed, the frequency of Alex's requests increased, and Sarah found herself juggling her workload with Alex's own. Often, she would stay late at work to meet deadlines, whereas Alex always left work early. He always had a networking event to catch or traffic to beat. Sarah was overwhelmed, but she didn't want the team to form a different perception of her.

One evening, Sarah had lunch with a friend who was a psychology major in college. This friend noticed how exhausted she was and asked what the problem was. Feeling the need to vent, Sarah poured out every single frustration about her work. After listening attentively,

Sarah's friend gently pointed out that Alex had been covertly manipulating her with underhanded tactics. He had been exploiting Sarah's need for professional validation to subtly shift his responsibilities onto her while getting all the benefits of her hard work.

This was a wake-up call for Sarah. Thinking back, she started recognizing how Alex had manipulated her into doing his work. Understandably, she felt betrayed and angry. At the same time, she resolved to break free from Alex's manipulation and reclaim her professional identity.

Now aware, Sarah began to set firm boundaries. Whenever Alex tried to make her take on a task meant for him, she would politely say, "I appreciate how confident you are in me, Alex, but I have a lot on my plate, too." with a smile. Alex was taken aback by Sarah asserting herself. He was used to her being compliant.

He tried guilt-tripping her by implying she was letting the team down. He even accused her of not being a team player. But Sarah remained steadfast and professional. She didn't argue or give in to the emotional manipulation. Instead, she learned to redirect their conversations to relevant work matters every time.

Interestingly, as Sarah reclaimed her time and energy, Alex's shortcomings became more apparent to everyone at the office. Because she no longer covered for him, he started making mistakes and missing deadlines. Eventually, their boss noticed the disparity in workload and efficiency, and Alex was fired.

Through this experience, Sarah learned a professional lesson and achieved personal growth. She learned to recognize subtle and obvious manipulation tactics, trust her instincts, set boundaries, and confidently assert herself. This earned her newfound respect from her coworkers and boss.

To understand dark psychology and its techniques, you first need to understand your emotions and those of others. The next chapter will teach you how to do this.

CHAPTER TWO:

Emotional Control For Achieving Influence

In the quest to become a master of dark psychology, there's something you must learn: the power of emotional control. By this, I mean the ability to control your emotions and those of others. In psychology, this ability is known as emotional intelligence. It entails recognizing, understanding, and influencing emotions, whether in yourself or others. Studies have shown that emotional intelligence is a valuable and rare asset that can help you develop relationships, improve job satisfaction, and defuse conflicts.

Most people often fall into the trap of giving completely emotional responses to the actions of others. Unfortunately, this plays right into others' hands, giving them the upper hand. If you want to be able to change people's thoughts and actions, that's something you can't afford. As such, you must learn and cultivate emotional control.

Imagine a scenario where a competitor does something you don't like. Your instinct might be to react angrily, giving your emotions the lead. But this is merely a knee-jerk reaction, and it's probably what that person was hoping for.

Letting people lure you into reacting emotionally gives them control over the situation while you become the pawn. Your emotions take over judgment, hindering your ability to be strategic and rational.

Of course, you don't want to be this kind of person. You want to be someone with emotional mastery. This is the key to influencing or manipulating others. Emotions are like a double-edged sword. Instead of allowing yourself to be controlled by your feelings, you learn how to do that to people. In other words, you must learn to control people through their emotions.

You need to know the basics about emotions and emotional intelligence to do this.

Understanding Emotions and Emotional Intelligence (EI)

Emotions impact our thoughts and behavior. They influence our small and big decisions and can compel us to take action. Sometimes, emotions last long, such as sadness at the end of a relationship. Other times, they are short-lived, like when you're briefly annoyed at a colleague at work.

You must understand the three main components to truly understand your and other people's emotions. Each component affects how you react or respond to your feelings. The three components include:

Emotions are typically understood to consist of three main components:

1. **Physiological**: This refers to how your body reacts to an emotion. It involves the bodily changes that occur in response to an emotional trigger, such as increased heart rate, sweating, or adrenaline release. An emotion's physiological component is automatic and depends on how intense the emotion is.
2. **Subjective**: This refers to how you experience an emotion internally and personally, including the psychological feeling. It encompasses the quality, intensity, and perception of the emotion by you.
3. **Behavioral**: This may also be referred to as the expressive component. Emotions often trigger actions, i.e., behavioral responses. These include simple responses like facial expressions and gestures and more complex ones like

approach, avoidance, communication, etc. The behavioral component of emotion is subject to cultural norms, personal experiences, and the specific context in which the feeling arises.

These three components shape how we experience and express our feelings in different contexts.

Mastering emotions is all about learning to manage all three components. When you understand the body's physical response to various emotions (tense muscles, racing heart), the subjective experience (such as recognizing how you feel), and the potential behavioral response (withdrawal, lashing out), it becomes remarkably easier to control not just your emotional reactions, but those of others as well.

This means you can influence how people react to you instead of letting their feelings dictate their actions. For instance, if you know that a certain situation would make your partner angry, you can work on calming them down by reframing their perception (subjective experience) of the problem. This can lead to them responding calmly.

Emotions exist for many reasons, including:

- **Keeping You from Danger**

Emotions are crucial for safety and survival. They alert us to danger, making us avoid it. Emotions can also prepare us for action. The amygdala triggers emotional responses, preparing our bodies to handle seemingly threatening or dangerous situations. This can activate the body's fight-or-flight response, readying us to flee to safety or face danger. Emotions prompt quick actions that increase our chances of success and survival.

- **Helping Others Understand How You Feel**

When interacting with people, emotions help others understand how you feel. You can use emotional expressions, such as body language and facial expressions, to convey your feelings. Sometimes, you need to state your emotions directly. Telling your family or friends that you feel frightened, sad, happy, or excited provides them with important information to take action.

- **Providing Motivation**

Emotions can be a strong source of motivation. For example, worrying about a difficult exam might make you study harder to ensure a good grade. To avoid negative emotions and increase positive ones, you might seek activities that bring excitement, contentment, and happiness while avoiding situations that cause boredom, sadness, or anxiety. Emotions make you more likely to take action—anger can drive you to confront an issue, fear can make you flee a threat, and love can lead you to seek a partner.

- **Understanding Others' Emotions**

Just as your emotions give valuable information to others, the emotional expressions of those around you provide a wealth of social information. Social communication is essential in relationships and daily life. The ability to react to and interpret others' emotions helps you respond appropriately and build deeper, more meaningful relationships with family, loved ones, and friends. It also allows you to communicate effectively in various social situations, from managing a hot-headed employee to handling an angry customer. Understanding others' emotional displays helps you determine the best response.

- **Influencing Your Decisions**

Emotions significantly influence your decisions, from which political candidates you vote for to what you choose for lunch. Emotions play a major role even when you think rationality and logic guide your choices. Emotional intelligence – which involves understanding and managing your emotions – is key in decision-making. Anger or joy can prompt quick action, disgust can make you discard belongings, and fear can heighten your perception of risk.

The Power of Emotional Intelligence

Emotional intelligence is "the ability to perceive, interpret, demonstrate, control, evaluate, and utilize emotions to communicate effectively and constructively with others." It's important to know how to express and control emotions and, just as important, how best to comprehend, interpret, and respond to others' emotions with effectiveness.

We all know that not always the smartest individuals are the most fulfilled or successful in life. You may have seen individuals who are academically brilliant but not successful in their personal relationships, at work, or socially inept.

Your intelligence quotient (IQ) or intellectual ability is not the only factor needed to succeed in life. Although a person's IQ can help them get into college, their EQ will help them successfully manage their emotions and stress during their final exams. EQ and IQ are both important.

Key signs of emotional intelligence include:

- being able to identify and describe what someone else is feeling
- awareness of your and others' strengths and limitations
- being able to let go of mistakes or failures
- Willingness to accept and welcome change
- a strong curiosity about others
- being sensitive to others' feelings
- being able to manage emotions in challenging situations

Here are areas of life where emotional intelligence is most crucial:

Social health and relationships

When you are in tune with your emotions, it connects you to other individuals and the world around you. You can reduce stress, recognize friends from foes, use social communication to balance your nervous system, measure another individual's interest in you, and feel happy and loved with social intelligence. Being aware of and managing your emotions helps you express your feelings more effectively and understand those of others. This helps you build stronger relationships in your personal life and at work as it increases effective communication.

Your physical and mental health

If you find it hard to control your emotions, your stress is probably not being managed well, which can cause serious health issues. When stress is not properly controlled, it can increase blood pressure, contribute to infertility, suppress the immune system, speed up the process of aging, and increase a person's risk of having a heart attack or stroke. Stress management is a key part of improving emotional intelligence.

When emotions are uncontrolled, it leads to stress. This, in turn, can impair your mental health, making you vulnerable to depression and anxiety. Suppose you find it difficult to understand, manage your emotions, or get comfortable with people. In that case, it will be hard for you to build strong relationships. This can leave you feeling isolated and further worsen any mental health issues.

Your work or school performance

Emotional intelligence equips you with the necessary skills to motivate and lead people, navigate the complexities of the workplace, and become successful in your career. Many companies employ EQ testing before hiring for jobs as they consider emotional intelligence as important as technical ability.

Components of EI

According to research, emotional intelligence has four components: the ability to perceive emotions, reason using emotions, understand emotions, and manage emotions.

- **Emotional perception**: To understand emotions, you must learn to perceive them accurately. This means knowing all about the nonverbal signs of emotions, including facial expressions and body language.

- **Emotional reasoning** means using your emotions to facilitate critical thinking and cognitive activity. Your emotions can help you prioritize what to pay attention to and react to. As humans, we respond emotionally only to what garners our attention.
- **Emotional understanding**: Every emotion has a meaning and a message. If someone is angry, you must be able to identify the cause of their anger and what it means. Let's say a client is expressing anger; it could mean they are dissatisfied with you or might have had a fight with their spouse on the way to your meeting.
- **Emotional regulation**: This is the peak of emotional intelligence. Knowing how to regulate emotions to induce an appropriate response is crucial to emotional control.

Building Emotional Intelligence

You can learn emotional intelligence skills at any point in life. However, keep in mind that it's one thing to understand about something and another thing to apply it in your everyday life. You may know how to do something, but that doesn't mean you'll be able to. So, as you build emotional intelligence, you must practice the skills every day to sharpen them and master applying them in real scenarios.

There are four areas of emotional intelligence: Self-awareness, social awareness, self-management, and relationship management. Mastering each of these is the key to cultivating emotional intelligence.

Let's talk about them one by one.

Self-Awareness

The initial step to developing emotional intelligence is cultivating self-awareness. This is attunement to yourself and, more specifically, your emotional state. Staying in tune with your emotions and ever-changing emotional state is critical to understanding how your thoughts and actions are influenced by emotions.

Your early life experience can influence your current emotional experience and attachment style. How you handle core feelings of fear, sadness, anger, and joy depends on the stability and quality of your early emotional experiences in your early life.

Suppose you had a primary caretaker when you were an infant who valued and understood your emotions. In that case, there is a high probability that your feelings will be valuable in adulthood. But suppose you had confusing, threatening, or painful emotional experiences as an infant. In that case, you most likely have learned to ignore or suppress your emotions.

- Do you often experience feelings that flow, moving from one emotion to another as your experiences change from moment to moment?
- Do physical sensations in places like your chest, throat, or stomach accompany your emotions?
- Do you have individual emotions and feelings, such as fear, joy, anger, and sadness, each of which can be seen in subtle facial expressions?
- Can you experience intense and strong feelings to capture your and other people's attention?
- Do you focus on your emotions? Do they contribute to the decisions you make?

You may even have turned them down if you are not paying attention to your emotions. If you want to become emotionally healthy and develop your EQ, you need to reconnect to your core emotions, embrace them, and be comfortable with them. Practicing mindfulness can help you achieve this.

What is mindfulness?

Mindfulness entails concentrating on the present moment and paying attention to it without judgment. If you are preoccupied with a thought, mindfulness helps you shift from that state of preoccupation toward a state of appreciation for the moment and your emotional and physical sensations. It also gives you a larger perspective on life. Mindfulness focuses and calms you, thereby increasing your self-awareness.

Social Awareness

Social awareness helps you recognize the mainly nonverbal cues other individuals constantly use to communicate and interpret them with you. These cues help you know what is important to others, their changing emotional state, and their feelings.

You have empathy. You can understand other people's needs, emotions, and concerns. You can recognize the power dynamics in an organization or group. You can pick up on emotional cues.

When groups of people send out similar nonverbal cues, social awareness allows one to read the cues and understand the group's shared emotional experiences and power dynamics. Thus, one becomes socially comfortable and empathetic.

Mindfulness is an ally of social and emotional awareness. To develop social awareness, the importance of mindfulness in the social process must be recognized. After all, it will be difficult to pick up on subtle nonverbal cues when you are zoning out on your phone, thinking about other things, or simply in your head. You need to be present in the moment to be socially aware.

Although many people are happy about the ability to multitask, this means that you won't notice the subtle emotional shifts in other individuals that make it easy for you to completely understand them. Your social goals will more likely progress when you put your thoughts aside and stay focused on the interaction itself.

When you follow the flow of another individual's emotional responses, you must also focus on the changes taking place in your emotional experience, as the process is a give-and-take.

Your self-awareness is not diminished when you pay attention to other people. When you put in effort and time to pay attention to other individuals, you will better understand your beliefs, values, and emotional state. For instance, if hearing others express certain views makes you uncomfortable, it opens your eyes to something important about yourself.

Self-Management (Self-Regulation)

You manage your emotions in healthy ways, control impulsive behaviors and feelings, adapt to changing circumstances, and follow through on commitments that you have started. Unfortunately, chronic stress can make you unable to control your emotions and find it difficult to act appropriately and thoughtfully.

Think about it: Has there been any time in your life when you have been overwhelmed with stress? Were you able to think clearly or avoid making an irrational decision? It must have been difficult to do this.

When stress overwhelms you, your ability to properly assess your emotions and those of others and to think becomes compromised.

Emotions are important when it comes to telling you about yourself and others, but that leads us out of our comfort zone when stressed. Emotions can overwhelm us, making us unable to control ourselves.

When you can manage your stress and remain present emotionally, you can master receiving upsetting information without allowing it to affect your self-control and thoughts. You will easily make choices that enable you to control impulsive behaviors and feelings, take initiative, manage your emotions healthily, adapt to changing circumstances, and follow through on commitments.

Relationship Management

You know what to do to develop good relationships and maintain them. You also know how to manage conflict, work well in a team, communicate effectively, and influence and inspire others. Your ability to recognize other people's feelings and understand their experiences helps you work well with people.

Emotional awareness is important when working with concerned people. You can successfully develop additional emotional and social skills that will help you form more fruitful, effective, and fulfilling relationships.

You must become aware of your nonverbal communication and its effectiveness. You are constantly sending nonverbal messages to people about your feelings and thoughts. The facial muscles, especially those around the forehead, nose, eyes, and mouth, help you read other people's emotional intent and convey your emotions without using words.

The emotional area of the human brain is always on, and other people won't ignore the messages it is sending, even if you ignore the messages. Your relationships can be greatly improved when you start paying attention to and recognizing the nonverbal messages you send to others.

Ensure that you see conflict as an opportunity to help you grow closer to others. Disagreements and conflict are inevitable in relationships. Two individuals can't possibly have the same expectations, opinions, and needs every time. Having the same or different expectations, opinions, and needs should not be bad. Trust can be strengthened when conflict is resolved in constructive and healthy ways. Safety, creativity, and freedom in relationships are encouraged when conflict is not seen as punishing or threatening.

Remember, I said that emotions play a role in decision-making. Let's find out what this means.

The Role of Emotions in Decision Making

The average person believes emotions are an obstruction to the decision-making process and, therefore, thinks they are better off without them. Rather than feeling, processing, and understanding their emotions, they actively try to suppress or ignore them. They would rather be rational than emotional. But the reality is that emotions will always factor into the decision-making process no matter how hard they try.

In your attempts to influence or persuade others, you might have mistakenly believed that all you need is to present them with facts. You think they will absorb your message and act accordingly if you make a rational argument. You do this based on the assumption that humans are inherently rational and logical. This is wrong – humans aren't completely rational. One might say that most people are more emotional than rational.

Humans are wired in such a way that things evoke emotions in us. Emotions are ever present in our thinking. Even facts evoke varying emotions in us. If you never consider this, your chances of influencing, persuading, or manipulating people's thoughts and actions will be slim.

Emotional influences constantly skew and determine the outcome of many daily decisions. Therefore, to influence or control those decisions, you must know all you can about emotions' role in decision-making.

But if you're not sold on this and still believe it's possible to influence people without using their emotions, let me tell you how emotions are formed and become actionable feelings.

First, every emotion has a trigger, an external stimulus. This could be a physical event or something someone said or did. That stimulus creates an emotion in the brain, causing the body to release responsive hormones. The hormones, in turn, go into the bloodstream and evoke feelings, which can be positive or negative. So, it's trigger > emotion >

hormones > feelings. From this, it becomes obvious that emotions affect decision-making by evoking certain feelings.

In essence, emotions are designed to inform our decisions. They condense our experiences and evaluate them so we can rapidly respond appropriately. Without them to motivate and push us, we would live passively, doing nothing.

Though emotions exist to guide us, they are automated. As such, the messages from our feelings are often conveyed below the level of conscious awareness. This means our emotions influence our decisions on a subconscious level. We think we're making an informed decision based on facts, but our emotions direct us.

You've probably had moments where you just "felt" like doing something, even when it didn't seem logical. That's emotions at work. When deciding on something minor or major, your emotions provide input based on mood, values, and past experiences.

Think about it: How often do you make snap decisions due to anxiety or excitement? Those feelings steer you toward specific choices. For instance, feeling excited about a new opportunity makes you likely to take a risk on it. In contrast, you might go for a safer option if you feel anxious.

One thing about emotions is that they aren't always big and obvious. Most times, they are subtle and creep on us. Suppose you have a choice between two job offers. The first one pays more, whereas the other makes you feel appreciated. You may not consciously acknowledge it, but that feeling can heavily influence your final choice. Of course, this also depends on what matters to you – money or validation.

Also, emotions add depth to the thinking process. Yes, rational thinking helps to analyze facts and figures, but emotions offer insight into your values. This enables you to assess the advantages and disadvantages of a decision more thoughtfully.

Here's where things get interesting: Due to how powerful they are, emotions can cloud judgment. That's why some people get angry, do something rash, and regret it later. Strong emotions appeal to our impulses, leading to instinctual reactions. This is where the key to controlling people with their emotions lies.

To control people's thoughts and actions, you must learn to evoke strong emotions. More importantly, you must ensure they remain unaware of how those feelings influence them.

How do you do that?

The answer is in the next chapter, where we will examine different ways to evoke and exploit powerful emotions in people.

Story

Let's talk about Jessica, a young woman who recently discovered the impact of emotional intelligence on her personal and professional life.

Jessica was bright, ambitious, and driven, but she struggled to connect with others emotionally like many people. However, once she mastered emotional intelligence, it transformed her career and relationships in ways her mind never imagined.

Jessica worked at a fast-paced marketing firm. She was highly skilled and great at her job and always delivered high-quality work. Despite all this, she wasn't moving up the ladder as quickly as one might expect. This was baffling. After all, she was punctual, organized, and did everything right—or did she?

One afternoon, after a particularly tasking meeting in which her ideas were once again dismissed, Jessica decided to seek advice from her mentor, Donna. Donna was a veteran professional with exceptional people skills. Jessica always wondered how Donna managed to handle even the trickiest situations smoothly. She also wished she knew how to say the right things like Donna.

Frustrated, Jessica confides in her mentor, saying, "I don't get it, Donna. I work so hard but I'm hardly making any progress in my career. What am I doing wrong?" Karen smiles gently and says, "Jessica, you're incredibly talented. But have you ever heard about emotional intelligence?"

Jessica was confused. What did emotional intelligence have to do with her lack of career growth? Donna then talked to her about emotional intelligence—why it helps to understand one's emotions and those of others and know how to manage them. She explained to Jessica that human interactions are all about empathy, effective communication, and building strong relationships, which are some of the components of emotional intelligence. Donna told Jessica that emotional intelligence is the key to her personal and professional growth.

Intrigued, Jessica decided to learn more about this concept. She read books, participated in workshops, and gradually started applying what she learned. Slowly, she observed changes in her interactions with other people. She improved at listening attentively to others, hearing their words and the emotions behind them. She became better at controlling her reactions and staying calm under pressure.

A few weeks after this, Jessica's boss called a meeting. It was a brainstorming session for their biggest client, and tensions ran high. Everyone was shooting ideas left and right, and the atmosphere was quite heavy. Jessica noticed a colleague, Mike, looking anxious – like he had something to say but was hesitant.

Instead of imposing her ideas as usual, she decided on a different approach. "Mike, I can see you're passionate about this project," she said calmly and understandingly. What's your perspective? I'd love to hear more about your ideas."

Mike was pleasantly surprised. He eagerly shared his thoughts while everyone else listened intently. Jessica, in particular, expressed genuine interest. This act of empathy was simple but powerful enough to change the meeting's entire dynamic. Other team members started engaging more openly, and soon, they collaborated and merged ideas. The meeting was fruitful, and it made Jessica happy.

Her growing emotional intelligence wasn't just benefiting her at work, though. She felt the impact even in her personal life. In the past, she used to have frequent petty arguments with her younger sister. They would fight over the most mundane stuff despite loving each other dearly. One evening, after another fight over borrowed shoes, Jessica decided to chat with her sister.

First, she apologized for getting upset because she was more caught up in her feelings than understanding how her sister felt. Her sister was quite surprised. Surely, this can't be the same Jessica! Both of them sat down and had an open, honest conversation. And they felt truly connected for the first time in a long while.

The change in Jessica's behavior didn't go unnoticed back at work. Her boss, Lisa, called her into the office one afternoon. "Jessica, I've noticed a significant change in you recently. You're not just doing your job; you're enhancing the team's dynamic. Your ability to connect with others and manage stress is remarkable. I'd like to promote you to team lead."

Jessica was thrilled. Her hard work, coupled with her honing emotional intelligence skills, had finally been rewarded. She became an effective leader and built a bridge of trust and cooperation within her team.

This story is a powerful example of how emotional intelligence transcends mere buzzwords. If honed right, it can transform all aspects of your life, and more importantly, it can give you power and influence over others.

In the next chapter, let's discuss techniques for exploiting people's emotional states.

CHAPTER THREE:

Techniques For Exploiting Powerful Emotions

Imagine yourself as a skilled chef creating a dish. A professional chef carefully selects the best ingredients, knowing each one's unique properties. In covert persuasion, understanding emotions is key. You need to read subtle emotional cues – body language, tone of voice, and facial expressions. This helps you identify what people are feeling and thinking without them explicitly saying it. Recognizing these unspoken emotions allows you to tailor your approach to align with their current emotional state.

As a chef balances flavors to create a harmonious dish, you must balance your responses to people's emotions. If someone feels anxious, you offer reassurance. If they're excited, you match their enthusiasm. This subtle alignment builds trust and rapport, making the person more receptive to your influence. By mirroring their emotions, you create a sense of understanding and connection.

A chef uses precise techniques to cook ingredients perfectly. Effective communication is a key technique for covert persuasion or manipulation. Using emotional intelligence, you can frame your words and actions in a way that subtly influences others. For example, a calm and steady tone can make you seem more trustworthy. In contrast, slight changes in your speech pattern can make your suggestions seem more appealing and reasonable.

Chefs taste and adjust their dishes to achieve the perfect balance. Similarly, you must be attuned to feedback and ready to adapt. If you sense resistance, you subtly change your approach – perhaps offering more empathy or shifting your arguments. Emotional intelligence allows you to perceive these subtle shifts and respond in a way that continues to guide the person toward your desired outcome without overt pressure.

Finally, a chef knows that presentation can make a dish irresistible. In covert persuasion, how you present your message is crucial. Using emotional intelligence, you can frame your ideas in a way that resonates emotionally. This might mean highlighting benefits that appeal to their desires or fears, using storytelling to create an emotional connection, or presenting your suggestions as their ideas. The goal is to make your influence feel natural and appealing, not forced.

The point is that honing your emotional intelligence enables you to subtly steer people's thoughts and actions without revealing your intentions. Just like a chef creates a delicious dish by understanding and balancing flavors, you can influence others by understanding and balancing their emotions. This makes changing their thoughts and actions much more effective and seamless.

Understanding this is fundamental to influencing or controlling people through their emotions. Let's discuss the most powerful emotions for covertly influencing, persuading, or controlling others.

Four Powerful Emotions for Changing Thoughts and Actions

You experience a wide range of emotions throughout your lifetime. Every emotion, to an extent, influences your decision-making process. But certain core emotions are much more impactful than others. They are emotions that you're quite familiar with. If you learn to evoke these emotions in people, it'll be easier to change their thoughts, which will, in turn, change their actions.

What are these emotions?

1. Fear

Fear is a primal emotion tied to survival. It activates the human survival instinct. As such, it can motivate us to take immediate action in the face of a threat—perceived or real—or danger. Fear is arguably the most powerful emotion for changing behavior. People will change their behavior if they see that choosing otherwise won't benefit them.

Fear evokes an unpleasant feeling of dread over the unknown. When a person is feeling fearful, they find it harder to interpret cues and context accurately. They don't know whether the situation is stable or evolving, which leads to impulsive decision-making. Also, fear makes them less confident in their decision-making skills. This can make them come to you (or someone else) for advice. When you're afraid, you go into survival mode, thus taking less time to carefully consider the potential outcomes.

Using fear: To use fear to control another person, you must present a clear and immediate threat to their well-being or survival. In other words, they should be shown what they stand to lose if they don't change that behavior. Then, you must provide a solution to eliminate or reduce the potency of the threat. Let them see how your idea will solve their problem, which will remove their fear.

Basically, present them with a scenario in which they must act immediately to prevent a bad situation from happening. This will let you influence their decision or action.

Example: Let's say you have a team member who regularly misses their deadlines. You've tried talking to them to no avail. Instead of threatening them directly, remind them of the severe consequences of missing their deadlines. You might say, "If you don't complete this task in time, we might lose our biggest client, which will lead to job cuts."

In this scenario, you evoke a feeling of fear by highlighting the possibility of losing a client and having job cuts. Out of fear of losing their job, the team members will feel compelled to prioritize and meet the deadline. This plays on their instinctual desire to avoid negative outcomes.

2. Anger

Anger ranks among the most intense emotions that humans can experience. It often provokes such strong reactions that we view it negatively. However, anger is a normal response to perceived unfairness or injustice. We feel angry when someone or something has violated our boundaries or rights.

Due to its intensity, anger can be a powerful motivator for change. It can energize a person to take action to correct a perceived wrong. That's why social justice movements use anger to gather and motivate their supporters.

Using anger: The key to controlling people's actions with anger is to highlight something unfair or unjust about their situation and use that to spur them to action. You must channel their anger toward what you want them to do. Show them a clear target for the anger and provide actionable steps.

Example: Suppose you want a business to support your proposal against their competitor. In that case, highlight how the competitor's unethical practices could harm the business's reputation and success. You might say, "You need to act now to stop them from unfairly dominating the market and putting your hard work to shame!"

In this scenario, framing the competitor's unethical practices and domination as a threat taps into the business' sense of fairness and competitiveness, provokes anger, and galvanizes them to action. It increases the chances of them supporting your proposal.

3. Sadness

Sadness is emotional pain characterized by a sense of loss, disadvantage, helplessness, disappointment, despair, and sorrow. It evokes feelings of empathy and compassion, prompting the sad person to take action to alleviate their own or someone else's suffering.

Sadness also instills a sense of urgency to avoid further loss or damage.

This is why nonprofit charity organizations typically share stories of those in need to evoke sadness and compel action. For example, an ad for a child sponsorship program may display the difficult conditions kids in poverty face to encourage donations from viewers.

When a person is sad, it impairs their decision-making process. Sadness fogs the brain, making the simplest, most routine decisions seem harder. This can make them turn to you for guidance, leaving them susceptible to your influence.

Also, sadness influences decision-making based on short-term gains. When a person is sad, they want to be happy again as quickly as possible. They might do whatever it takes, regardless of the long-term consequences.

Finally, sadness can cause people to undervalue themselves and their possessions. In a study in which participants were made to feel sadness and then asked to set a price for an item, the sad participants set a lower price than the neutral participants.

Using sadness: To use sadness to change people's minds, you have to tell a compelling story to evoke that emotion and their empathy. Then, show them the negative consequence of not taking action and how a specific action (the one you want) can make a difference.

Example: If you want a friend to help with your school project, you might narrate how hard you've worked and how disappointed your parents will be if you don't succeed. You might say, "My parents have put so much effort and money into my education despite their low wages, and if I fail, they might never recover emotionally."

In this scenario, your story conveys deep emotional investment and vulnerability about the possibility of failure. This can evoke sadness and empathy, which prompt a desire to alleviate your distress in the other person. It can spur them to lend their support to facilitate your project's success.

4. **Guilt**

Guilt is a manipulator's second favorite emotion to use against other people. Fear is the first. People who are skilled at dark psychology techniques often use fear and guilt together as manipulation tools.

Guilt is a powerful emotional response tied to our sense of right and wrong. People feel guilty when they do something that conflicts with their values or moral standards. Feelings of guilt can range from mild regret to intense remorse. As such, individuals will change their behavior to avoid the feeling of guilt or make amends.

Using guilt: If you appeal to a person's sense of empathy or moral code, you can control their behavior or gain sympathy. This is called guilt-tripping. It involves making others feel morally responsible for your needs and desires. This will compel them to change their behavior (or do whatever else they want) to avoid feeling responsible for unfulfilled needs.

Example: If you want a romantic partner to help with something, you might remind them of past favors and subtly let them know you'll be disappointed if they don't reciprocate. You might say, "I've always been there for you, and now that I need you, I truly hope you can do the same."

In this scenario, referencing past favors makes them feel indebted and guilty for not repaying you in kind – even if they have a valid reason for not wanting to help. This pressures them into feeling obligated to help, even at their expense.

These aren't the only emotions you can exploit to change people's minds and behavior, but they are the most powerful.

Next, let's discuss how to read people's emotions accurately.

Reading People's Emotions

Many think communication is merely an exchange of information via words. However, nonverbal communication, exchanging information with the face and body, is just as important. Some experts even argue that the latter is more important.

Some people are skilled at reading emotions through nonverbal clues. They don't need you to tell them how you feel; they'll figure it out through your body language. Not everyone can do this, but the good news is that you can learn, practice, and hone this skill.

Body language comprises the nonverbal signals we use for communication, consciously or subconsciously. It makes our message more impactful and reveals our true feelings. According to research, body language accounts for 60 to 65 percent of all communication. That's how much we use our bodies to convey information.

You don't have to study psychology or psychiatry to master the ability to read people's emotions through their body language. If you want to read people's minds, you'll need superpowers. When I say "read people's emotions," I mean accurately intuiting what they think and feel. You might not always get it right, but you will most of the time.

Reading others' feelings requires identifying cues conveyed through facial expressions, gestures, body movements, posture, eye gaze, and vocal tone. Facial expressions are micromotor movements activated by unfelt emotions in the brain. To analyze and interpret a person's facial expression accurately, you must focus on every facial movement. The aim is to learn how they feel through nonverbal information.

For instance, if a friend starts yawning during your interaction, this could cue boredom, disinterest, or fatigue. It signals that it's time to change the subject or end the conversation.

The brain plays a critical role in deciphering nonverbal signals, such as microexpressions. The largest brain regions are responsible for interpreting everything we see.

The brain's "visual system" comprises every part of the brain that helps to interpret nonverbal cues. This system is in the occipital lobe, the lower back of the brain. It works with the amygdala and other brain areas. For example, when you look at someone's face, the amygdala produces electric signals known as spikes in response. The Fusiform gyrus and the amygdala work together as the brain's face perception network.

Inside the amygdala, there are emotion-tracking neurons that help detect a person's emotional intensity, i.e., how strongly they feel an emotion. On the other hand, the ambiguity-coding neurons indicate how ambiguous an emotion feels.

Interpreting Body Language

Examples of body language are a head tilt showing that you are thinking, arm and hand movements to demonstrate directions or an upright stance to show interest. It can also be tapping your feet restlessly or taking care to avoid an arms-crossed posture that is defensive.

When you read these signs, you can fully understand what a person is telling you. Your awareness of people's reactions to what you say and do will increase. You will also know how to adjust your body language to appear more approachable, engaging, and positive.

Knowing how to interpret people's body language to understand them and communicate with them more effectively will help you greatly in your personal and professional relationships. When communicating their true feelings, an individual's body language is more important than their choice of words and tone of voice.

When you are aware of people's body language, you can pick up on unspoken reactions and emotions. Reading people's body language is important, but you can miss it if you don't know what to look for.

Let's look at common examples of negative body language. If an individual exhibits these negative behaviors, they might be unhappy, disinterested, and disengaged.

- If an individual has their eyes downcast or maintains very little contact.
- If their arms are folded in front of their body.
- If their body is turned away from you.
- If they have tense or minimal facial expressions.
- Biting of nails, which suggests stress or insecurity.
- Fidgeting, which suggests that a person is distracted or disinterested.
- Blinking rapidly, indicating concern or uncertainty.
- Locked ankles, also connected to anxious thoughts.
- Tapping/drumming fingers is often a sign of boredom or impatience.

When you are aware of the meaning of these signals, it can help you adjust what you say and how you say it. If someone shows signs of being unhappy, you can show empathy for their unhappiness. You can work to calm a heated situation or explain yourself more clearly.

If a person shows these signs during a negotiation, you should focus on putting the person at ease and engaging their interest. Then, if the person stops displaying negative behavior, you will know that they are more open to persuasion and are ready to negotiate effectively with you.

Some types of body language show that a person is bored by what you tell them. This might be in a one-on-one chat, a team meeting, or a presentation.

Some popular signs of boredom include:

- Doodling or writing can be noticed in some individuals.
- Picking at clothes, fidgeting, or fiddling with phones and pens.
- Gazing into space or at something else.

- Sitting slumped, with head downcast.

People also convey positive feelings through their body language. Positive emotions can include happiness, interest, and trust. Seeing these signs lets you know that others are engaged with what you tell them and are at ease with the situation. If you mirror these body language cues, you can avoid sending mixed signals, convey your ideas more clearly, and support your points.

Meanwhile, you can use body language to influence people's perception of you. Let's say you want to make a good first impression. Your body language plays a big role in people's first impressions of you. You can appear engaged, trustworthy, calm, and confident by doing the following:

- **Avoid fiddling with your hair, touching your face, or scratching your nose**. If you answer questions and do this, it might be taken as a sign of dishonesty. You need to convey trustworthiness, so avoid doing any of that. Sincere smiles are infectious, reassuring, and attractive.
- **Your posture should be open**. You should be relaxed and ensure that you don't slouch. Sit or stand upright, and your hands should be placed by your sides. Ensure that you don't put your hands on your hips while standing, as this can communicate a desire to dominate and aggression.
- **Give a firm handshake, but don't overdo it**. It should not become aggressive, awkward, or painful for the other individual.
- **Maintain eye contact for a few seconds at an interval**. This will help the other person know that you are engaged and sincere. Don't overdo it to avoid making it a staring contest. Hold their gaze for a few seconds at a time.

Body language plays different important roles in interpersonal interactions. It facilitates trust, emphasizes a point, reveals underlying truths, and attunes to people's needs. Remember that your interpretations of a person's nonverbal cues may not always be accurate.

As you learn to manipulate others through their emotions, it's best to watch out for when others might be trying to manipulate you emotionally. That way, you can resist their attempts.

Resisting Emotional Manipulation

Knowing how to defend yourself against emotional manipulation from others is a key aspect of mastering dark psychology. Even as you learn to use people's emotions to influence their actions, you must take steps to protect your emotional well-being. This is key to maintaining your autonomy.

Emotional manipulators might evoke guilt to make you feel responsible for their happiness, anger to bully you, fear to intimidate you, or sadness to elicit your sympathy. Remember, the goal is to make you do whatever they want.

To resist emotional manipulation, you must learn to recognize when it’s happening. Common signs include:

- **Inconsistent behavior**: The manipulator's behavior might be unpredictable, swinging from overly friendly to hostile.
- **Guilt-tripping**: They make you feel responsible for their problems or unhappiness.
- **Intimidation**: They use overt or subtle threats to make you comply.
- **Playing the victim**: They exaggerate their misfortunes to gain your sympathy and assistance.
- **Withholding information**: They give you partial information to mislead you and control the narrative.

Once you recognize signs of emotional manipulation, resisting it becomes as easy as learning ABC. Follow these steps to protect your emotions from people's influence:

- **Maintain self-awareness**. Recognize your emotions and understand why you're feeling them. Are you genuinely at fault, or is someone trying to make you feel guilty?
- **Set clear boundaries**. Clearly define what you're comfortable with and communicate these boundaries firmly. For instance, "I can't lend you money. Please respect my decision."
- **Stay calm**. Manipulators often try to provoke a strong emotional reaction. Stay calm, take deep breaths, and think logically about the situation.
- **Ask questions**. Challenge the manipulator's statements by asking clarifying questions. This can expose their tactics and make them reconsider their approach. For example, "Why do you think it's my responsibility?"
- **Seek support**. Talk to trusted friends, family, or a counselor about your experiences. They can provide an outside perspective and support your efforts to resist manipulation.

Here are specific examples of emotional manipulation and how to resist it.

Fear

- **Example**: A coworker says, "If you don't stay late to complete this project, the entire team may fail, and the responsibility could fall on you."
- **Response**: Calmly assess the situation. "I understand the deadline is important, but I have commitments outside of work. Let's discuss how we can manage this task together."

Anger

- **Example**: A friend yells at you for not agreeing to their plan, saying, "You never support me!"
- **Response**: Stay calm and set limits. "I won't continue this conversation if you raise your voice. Let's talk when we're both calm."

Sadness

- **Example**: A family member says, "I'm so depressed that you're not coming to visit. If you cared, you'd be here."
- **Response**: Recognize the manipulation and offer empathy without compliance. "I'm sorry you're feeling this way. I can't visit right now, but I'm here to talk if you need to."

Guilt

- **Example**: A partner says, "If you loved me, you'd do this for me."
- **Response**: Acknowledge their feelings but stand your ground. "I care about you, but I also need to respect my own boundaries."

Resisting emotional manipulation means staying aware, setting boundaries, and protecting your emotional health. It's about recognizing when someone is trying to exploit your emotions and responding assertively and calmly.

If you learn to do this, you will maintain control over your actions and decisions at all times, ensuring they align with your values and well-being.

Story

Let me tell you about Lola. She's the kind of person who can read a room just by walking into it. She's got this uncanny ability to read people, almost like she's got a superpower. Ever noticed how some folks know exactly what to say to make you feel better or see things differently? That's Lola for you.

One time, at a family gathering, the atmosphere was thick with tension. Her cousin, Declan, had just gone through a rough breakup, and the whole family was walking on eggshells. Lola watched for a moment, reading the room. Then, she sat down next to Declan and started chatting. She didn't dive right into asking how he was; instead, she shared a funny story from their childhood. Before long, Declan was laughing, and the tension in his shoulders eased.

Lola's talent isn't just about talking; it's about listening, too. She pays close attention to body language – the slight droop of a shoulder, a forced smile, restless hands. These cues tell her more than words ever could. It's like she has a sixth sense of emotions.

What's even more impressive is how she handles emotional manipulation. We all have that one friend who tries to guilt-trip us or use flattery to get their way. But Lola? She sees right through it. Her friend, Jenna, often tried to manipulate Lola into canceling plans to hang out whenever Jenna was feeling lonely. With her kind yet firm approach, Lola made it clear that emotional manipulation wouldn't work on her. She gently but firmly reminded Jenna that their friendship was built on mutual respect and honesty.

Lola's knack for evoking emotions to influence thoughts and actions, combined with her skill at reading people's feelings and resisting manipulation, makes her remarkable. She shows us that understanding and managing emotions is a powerful tool that can foster positive change and stronger relationships.

We've briefly touched on emotional manipulation here. It's time to explore the art of manipulation in-depth in the next chapter. Find out how to become a master manipulator while protecting yourself from manipulation!

CHAPTER FOUR:
The Art Of Manipulation

You will have times when you don't get what you desire from people, but it doesn't mean you should be disappointed. Learn to manipulate the lemon salesperson when life gives you lemons. This is how to get what you want in life.

Sure, manipulating people is generally considered a bad thing. Depending on your goals, what you learn here can be used positively or to protect yourself from manipulation in your daily interactions. Know that you don't have to harm people with manipulation tactics. Remember the kitchen knife analogy – what you do with these techniques determines whether they are bad or good.

Manipulation is about influencing people to do whatever you want. This might sound sneaky, but it's prevalent in our daily encounters. You've had people change your mind a few times without realizing it – we all have. That's the art of manipulation at work.

At its core, manipulation requires a rudimentary understanding of human behavior. You need a keen sense of intuition and empathy to get what you want from people. Manipulation also involves a mix of social skills and psychological tactics. A skilled manipulator can read people's emotions, identify vulnerabilities, and anticipate reactions accurately. This is how they tailor their approach to each target. Some people are inherently skilled at it, whereas others learn over time.

When I say you must understand human behavior to manipulate effectively, what do I mean?

Emotional Intelligence

The best manipulators have very high emotional intelligence. They can identify and manage not just their emotions but those of other people as well. As you know, you need this skill to appropriately respond to different emotional states. This makes manipulation much more effective.

Nonverbal Cues

You must hone your ability to read body language, facial expressions, and vocal tone. Manipulation requires picking up on nonverbal cues, no matter how subtle. This is how you uncover a person's true feelings about anything, even if they don't explicitly communicate them.

Empathy and Sympathy

Empathy is putting yourself in someone else's shoes, while sympathy is feeling compassion for them. As a manipulator, you need cognitive empathy to understand what a person is going through and their needs or wants. Then, you must use this to demonstrate sympathy. That is how to establish a bond and gain their trust so that you can easily influence their thoughts and actions.

Social Dynamics

An understanding of social dynamics is key to the art of manipulation. You must know power structures, relationships, and unwritten rules within social groups. You need this knowledge to handle social situations smoothly. This is how the best manipulators position themselves to maximize their influence.

Behavioral Psychology

Knowing behavioral psychology principles, such as conditioning and reinforcement, can make you an advanced master in manipulation. You should know how to use positive reinforcement (rewards) or negative reinforcement (eliminating something unpleasant) to gradually shape people's behavior over time. This is how you play in the big leagues.

Anticipating Reactions

Humans have predictable reactions to certain stimuli. Individuals skilled at manipulation recognize these patterns, making predicting people's responses to varying statements and actions easier. With this foresight, they can make strategic moves to influence others, increasing their chances of achieving their desired outcomes.

Dependency

Making others dependent on you for emotional support, validation, approval, or resources is the key to long-term influence on their thoughts, feelings, actions, and decisions. Dependency ensures the target continues to seek your approval or support in whatever they do.

Flexibility

Finally, the most skilled manipulators are flexible. They can adapt their approach depending on the situation and the target. This flexibility is necessary to remain effective in different scenarios and with all kinds of individuals.

Based on these factors, the best way to influence people's behavior is to exploit their cognitive biases and vulnerabilities. Targeting these areas makes it incredibly easy to steer the average person toward an action or belief that will serve your interest. Why?

These are the weakest points that make humans susceptible to influence. They impair a person's ability to think rationally or act independently. If you play in any of these areas, you're more likely to achieve your personal goal.

The question is, how do you target these areas? Let me show you how.

Exploiting Cognitive Biases

Cognitive biases are systematic thinking errors that occur when we process and interpret information in the environment, subtly influencing our judgments and decisions. As powerful as the human brain is, it is subject to limitations. A cognitive bias is the product of the brain's attempt at simplifying information processing.

Think of cognitive biases as mental shortcuts to simplify decision-making. They help us make meaning and reach decisions with speed. As a result, biases affect how we perceive and think about the world and everyone in it.

There are hundreds of biases, but the most common and easiest to exploit for influencing people's decisions and behaviors include the following:

- **Confirmation Bias**

People tend to search for, interpret, and recollect information in a way that confirms their existing beliefs. They favor this approach. You can exploit this by presenting your target with selective information reinforcing their views or views.

For example, say you want to convince a customer to buy an expensive product. You might show them positive reviews from other customers with similar preferences, which can make them more confident about purchasing the product.

- **Anchoring Bias**

People make most decisions based on the first information they receive (the anchor). The key to exploiting the anchoring bias is to present your target with an initial piece of information that skews their perception of the situation. This lays the foundation for subsequent manipulation.

For example, as a real estate agent, you might first show a client a very expensive house to set a high price anchor. Subsequently, any house you show will seem reasonable by comparison, even if it's also costly.

- **Recency Bias**

This is a tendency to give greater importance to recent events over older ones. Recency bias affects how the brain perceives and interprets a situation. Since recent events are more prominent in the mind, people are more likely to remember them and give them more weight in decision-making.

Imagine you want your roommate to switch grocery stores. You have a crush on the new store, but it's far from your apartment. Your current store has recently had a few incidents of items being sold out and long check-out lines. In this case, you can exploit recency bias by reminding them of the recent incidents: "Remember last week when we had to wait forever in line? And just two days ago, they were out of milk again!" Then, share a positive experience with the new store: "I went to the new store yesterday, and it was so quick and fully stocked." This makes them more inclined to agree the new store is better, even if the old one has been mostly fine in the past.

- **Availability Bias**

This bias makes people overestimate the importance of readily available information. To manipulate someone using it, you might repeatedly expose them to specific ideas or information, making the idea seem more significant than it actually is.

Say you want a new partner to swap their preferred ridesharing service for yours. In that case, start bringing up unpleasant news or experiences with their ridesharing service. For instance, "Did you hear about that driver who got into an accident last week? It was with that service you use!" Every time they mention using the service, share a different bad incident. "My friend used that service last month and the car broke down halfway. It was a nightmare!" "I just read another article about a robbery in one of their cars." Doing this makes the risks seem more common than they are. Then, tell them you don't feel safe using the service anymore with everything happening.

The more you bring negative experiences to your partner's attention, the more likely they will overestimate the frequency and severity of the ridesharing service's problems. This could lead them to switch to your preferred service, believing it's safer and more reliable.

Exploiting Vulnerabilities

We all have vulnerabilities. By this, I mean things that make us feel weak or insecure. A person's vulnerabilities can be emotional, such as fears or anxieties, or situational, such as financial troubles. Vulnerabilities are part of being human.

One of the best ways to manipulate people is to take advantage of their vulnerabilities to influence or control their decisions. It involves targeting them where they are most insecure or sensitive.

Was there ever a time when you were extremely stressed about money? If someone came to you with an investment deal that seemed too good to be true, you might fall for it due to your financial status. That's what it means to exploit vulnerabilities. The person is attempting to use your money problems for personal gains at your expense.

Some of the most common vulnerabilities you can identify and target to make people do what you want include:

- **Need for Approval**

The need for approval is deeply ingrained in humans. Unfortunately, this need is stronger in some people than others. I mentioned earlier in this book that humans are wired for connection. We are social creatures, seeking others' approval to feel valued and accepted. This approval boosts self-esteem.

When you approve of someone or validate them, they feel good about themselves. This makes them more likely to comply with your requests. Also, some people have a strong fear of rejection and negative perceptions. They might seek approval to avoid the distress of being disliked.

The best way to exploit this need is to conditionalize your approval. This means offering validation only when the person does what you want. If you do this, it'll create a cycle where they constantly seek your approval. When you give validation as a reward, it reinforces the desired behavior. We call this positive reinforcement, and it's one of the most effective ways to shape someone's actions to your advantage.

- **Insecurities**

Insecurities are feelings of anxiety, uncertainty, or a lack of confidence about one's abilities or physical appearance. They stem from feeling inadequate, unlovable, or unworthy. Due to their personal and sensitive nature, it's easy to get what you want from people by targeting their insecurities.

A person's insecurities are tied to their emotions. When insecure about something, they tend to be emotional rather than logical. This makes them susceptible to manipulation. Also, insecure people usually overcompensate for their inadequacies by striving to prove themselves. You can take advantage of this.

For example, if you have a friend who is insecure about their financial status, you can encourage them to earn social acceptance by overspending on gifts. You might even praise them for being generous.

- **Loneliness**

Humans need companionship, and they become vulnerable when they don't have it. Thus, loneliness is a vulnerability that can be exploited for manipulation. Individuals alone or lonely are more willing to lower their standards or overlook red flags for interpersonal connections. Their desperation for social interactions makes them eager for attention from anyone. This, of course, makes it easy to establish a bond and build trust rapidly.

Additionally, loneliness can make people less critical of your intentions. They may not scrutinize your ideas or suggestions as closely as they should. Why? Because the mere thought of socializing lowers their defenses. Such a person might quickly divulge personal information that you can use to your advantage.

The surest way to exploit a person's loneliness is to offer them the attention and companionship they crave. First, shower them with lots of attention and affection to quickly form a bond. Then, you can use the connection to extract favors or influence their behaviors. If they don't comply, you might threaten to withdraw your affection. That always works.

Remember that the key to potent manipulation lies in combining these tactics. Doing this maximizes your influence and increases the potential of achieving the desired outcome.

So far, we've discussed the fundamentals of manipulation through biases and vulnerabilities. Now, it's time to discuss the most powerful techniques for exploiting human behavior.

Powerful Manipulation Techniques

The general idea is that psychopaths, sociopaths, and narcissists are the only people with mastery of manipulation techniques. People believe you must fall under any of these categories to be a master manipulator. However, this isn't necessarily true. Like anything, manipulation techniques can be learned and acquired.

What are manipulation techniques? They are strategies and tactics for influencing others without their awareness. They can be overt or covert, depending on the situation and the person using them.

How powerful a manipulation technique is depends on the subtlety, emotional impact, and the context in which you use it.

- **Subtlety**: Manipulation works best when the technique is hard to detect. This depends on how subtle the method is. People are less likely to resist if they don't know they're being influenced or manipulated. Gaslighting and flattery are some of the most subtle techniques for manipulation.

- **Emotional impact**: Techniques that appeal to intense emotions are generally more potent for manipulation. Fear, guilt, and love are the strongest motivators for changing people's behaviors.

  Context: The power of a manipulation technique also depends on the situation. For instance, fear-based manipulation is often more effective in high-stakes situations. In relationships, emotional manipulation works better due to the existing connection.

The most powerful manipulation techniques operate under the radar, evoke intense emotions, or fit the situation perfectly.

So, based on these factors, here are 10 of the most powerful techniques for manipulating people.

1. **Gaslighting**

That didn't happen. Are you crazy? You're imagining it.

These variations of the same three words are the best ways to encapsulate what gaslighting is. Gaslighting is one of the most insidious manipulation techniques to have in your toolkit because it helps to distort and gradually erode a person's sense of reality.

You try to make the target doubt their perception of what's real and what isn't. You make them question their memory by denying things you've said or done. If you've ever had someone insist you're misremembering an event despite your memory being very clear, that's a classic example of gaslighting.

To gaslight someone:

- **Deny and lie**: If they accuse you of doing or saying something, deny it completely.
- **Contradict their memory**: Double down on your denial by telling them they don't know what they're discussing. Insist they don't remember what you said or did right.

- **Persist**: You must wear down their confidence by constantly following the first two steps on different occasions. Over time, they will start to doubt their memory and perception.

The goal of gaslighting is to make the target dependent on your version of reality. They will rely on you to make decisions if they can no longer trust themselves.

For example, say your partner asks you to pick up some groceries on the way home, but you don't want that to become a habit. You might respond when they ask, "You never asked me to do that. Are you imagining things? Your memory seems off. Is everything okay?"

2. **Love bombing**

You're the best person I've ever known, even though it's only been three days. I'm seeing a future with you that I've never seen with anyone else.

Love bombing is when you bombard someone with attention, affection, and praise to quickly establish a bond with them. It's best used in the early phase of your relationship to win them over quickly. You must sweep them off their feet and prime them for your influence. To the target, love bombing seems like a positive thing. Still, for you, it sets the stage for using another manipulation technique on them.

To love to bomb a person:

- **Overwhelm them with attention**. Shower them with lavish gifts, compliments, and affection.
- **Create dependence**. The more you bomb them, the more they'll depend on your constant attention and validation. Give them more.
- **Withdraw and control**. Once the target is hooked, withdraw and make them desperate for your attention. Then, use that as leverage for influencing or controlling them.

For instance, let's say you start dating someone new. Within the first month of meeting, you might send them flowers daily, take them on lavish dates, frequently remind them how lucky you are to meet them and talk about your future together. They should be hooked within that timeframe. If you become distant from nowhere, that person will find themselves doing anything to get the initial attention back.

Love bombing works by exploiting people's need for approval and validation. It's best used with people who can't validate themselves.

3. Guilt-Tripping

This is when you make someone feel responsible for a situation by evoking guilt. Since guilt is a powerful motivator, you make them feel guilty and use that card to get them to change their behavior or take a desired action. One classic way to guilt-trip someone you're close with is to ask, "Did you ever really care about me? If you did, you'd do this for me."

Depending on the situation, you might rely on something the person already feels guilty about or evoke a sense of responsibility to manipulate their emotions.

To guilt-trip someone:

- **Play the victim**. Express sadness or disappointment over a situation.
- **Imply the person's responsibility**. Subtly suggest it's their fault or they had something to do with what went wrong.
- **Extract compliance**. They feel guilty, so they should do what they want to get rid of that feeling.

For example, you say to someone, "I was so sad and lonely last weekend because you didn't call. I guess I don't matter to you." They feel guilty and call you frequently, even when it's inconvenient.

4. Silent Treatment

This is a passive-aggressive manipulation technique that involves ignoring someone who wants your attention to make them feel isolated and helpless. These feelings can make them desperate for any form of communication and validation. You can use the silent treatment until the person agrees to do what you want.

To do this:

Withdraw communication: Suddenly, stop interacting with them. Ignore their presence when you're in the same room.

- **Create anxiety**: Make them worry about what they did wrong by refusing to talk about it.
- **Force compliance**: Let them know the only way to resume communication is to comply with your demands.

Suppose you've argued with a friend and want them to apologize – even though they weren't at fault. In that case, you might stop responding to their texts and calls. They might spend days stressing over what they did wrong and finally apologize profusely to get you to talk to them again.

5. **Play the Victim**

Sometimes, the best way to get what you want from people is to portray yourself as a victim, no matter the situation. This technique works by distracting your target from your faults and placing the focus on your "suffering." It's effective but should be reserved for situations where nothing else has worked. Otherwise, people might label you a perpetual victim.

To play the victim:

- **Exaggerate hardship**: Constantly talk about how hard your life is.
- **Shift blame**: Make it seem like known and unknown forces are out to get you.
- **Evade accountability**: The target may feel sorry for you and overlook what happened.

If you want a coworker to do your work, you might talk about how unfair the boss is toward you. Take it further by suggesting you might give up on the job. The coworker may start covering for you because they feel bad about your "tough situation."

6. Triangulation

This involves bringing a third party into a situation that affects you and another person, creating conflict. Triangulation is a great "divide and conquer" strategy. It's best used to make someone doubt their stance or decision. You might say things like, "So-and-so agree with me," to make them tense.

To use this technique:

- **Introduce a third party**. Bring someone you both know into the conversation or conflict.
- **Create division**. Share selective information about something the third party said to create tension between them and the other person.
- **Control the narrative**. Keep them off balance and let them come to you for the “truth.”

Imagine you have two close friends and want to be the one each friend is closest to. In that case, you might use triangulation by telling one friend, "So-and-so said you're being really difficult to hang out with lately." This friend might feel hurt and wonder why others would say such a thing about them. Give them a reason to control the narrative. While the first friend is upset, you might tell the other person the friend has been saying negative things about them, too.

In this example, triangulation sows mistrust between your friends. It keeps both of them dependent on you for information and mediation. You can stay in the middle and influence them.

7. Projection

Suppose you're ever in a situation where you want to evade accountability for wrongdoing. In that case, projection is one of the best techniques for you. It involves attributing your negative behavior, mistake, or failure to someone else to deflect and make them defensive. Putting them on the defensive makes them too distracted to focus on your faults. For example, you might accuse someone of being selfish if they notice that behavior in you.

To use projection:

- **Deny**: Don't acknowledge what you did.
- **Accuse**: Attribute that trait or behavior to the other person.
- **Deflect and distract**: Shift focus away from yourself by giving instances of when this person displayed that behavior or trait.

For example, you might accuse your partner of being selfish for wanting a night out with friends, even though you frequently do the same without considering their plans. They'll end up defending themselves instead of talking about your selfishness.

8. Mirroring

This involves mimicking your target's behavior, interests, and speech patterns to establish rapport and trust quickly. They feel like they've met a kindred spirit because you're "just like them." This calculated move makes it easy to suggest things to them.

To mirror someone:

- **Observe**: Closely monitor your target's behavior, body language, facial expressions, gestures, interests, etc.
- **Mimic**: Start imitating all of these to form a connection. Imitate their likes and dislikes as well. For example, if they mention liking something, express the same interest. They will feel an instant bond and trust you.
- **Strike**: Use that leverage to covertly influence their thoughts, ideas, actions, decisions, etc.

You've just started working at a new place and want to build rapport. Your boss says they love hiking, so you tell them how much you love it, too. They mention that Bear Mountain is their favorite trail, so you say, "Wow, that's one of my favorite spots too. The blue trail has such a great view!" Meanwhile, you learned this from your cousin, who's a hiking enthusiast.

9. Diversion

Diversion is when you change the subject or dodge a question to avoid responsibility or keep the other person's balance. You might answer their question with another question or steer the conversation completely differently.

To divert:

- **Avoid direct answers**. If someone confronts you about something, dodge their question.
- **Change the subject**. Steer the conversation away from the topic by bringing up something completely different.
- **Keep them off balance**. Do not give a straight answer to leave them further confused and compliant.

Let’s say a coworker asks why you missed a crucial deadline. You might respond with, “Oh! "Have you seen the new project proposal? It’s really interesting." If they’re easy to distract, they will forget their original question.

10. Fear-Mongering

This manipulation technique uses scare tactics to influence decisions and behavior. By instilling fear, you can more effectively control actions and thoughts. "If you don't do this, something bad will happen."

To use fear-mongering:

- **Exaggerate**: Make something seem more dangerous than it is.
- **Instill fear**: Give examples to make them anxious and scared.
- **Control**: Direct them to make choices out of that fear.

For example, if you’re an insurance sales rep, you might tell a customer, "If you don’t invest in this insurance, your family could be left with nothing if something happens to you." In response, they might feel scared and agree to the investment out of fear.

These are some of the most powerful manipulation techniques. Here are some tips to make using these manipulation techniques significantly easier:

- **Become a master of emotions.**

As I explained in the second chapter, playing with people's emotions is the easiest way to manipulate them. If you give people enough time to think about something, they will likely make a logical decision. However, if you manipulate them into feeling a certain way that benefits you, it will be easy for you to get what you want from them.

Ideally, the person you are targeting won't have so much control over their emotions, but that shouldn't make you lazy. You need to be able to act since you are a master manipulator. You must master important skills, including getting angry when it suits your needs or shedding a tear. Whether you are looking for sympathy, you want to incite fear, or anything else you want to do, it will depend on the situation you want to handle. So, mastering your emotions is important to give you the right tools for the task.

- **Learn to flirt often and be charming.**

You can't just throw tantrums or cry like children do whenever you need something. You have to be likable. Charm is necessary when it comes to manipulating individuals. If you are an individual who is ridiculously likable a lot of the time, reacting with extreme emotion will greatly impact the situation. When you can control your feelings, you can't just act, but you can keep your emotions in check most of the time.

Although a charming personality is great, having the ability to flirt can also be helpful. The target generally feels poorly when manipulated, whether or not they know they are being manipulated. The more the target likes you, the better things will flow. Disregard your own sexuality's boundaries and some suggestive touches can be thrown in when you believe that they will be effective. This works well with lonely individuals and those with low self-esteem.

- **Hide negative action in altruism.**

Even if you are not a good person, you have to seem like you are. If you need to take a negative action like blaming someone else, whether it's the person's fault or yours, yelling at the target, or even criticizing behavior, you should do your best to wrap it in altruism.

An altruist is not easily hated, so painting yourself as one is very effective. For instance, if your target didn't do what you wanted them to do and you yelled at them, you can frame the outburst as a way of helping the target. Apologize for the outburst and tell them you yelled at them because you felt they were not acting in their best interest.

You can say that you care about them, have their best interest at heart, and are sorry you got so emotional. Tell the person it worries you to think that the person does not have their best interest at heart.

On the other hand, you can remind a target when you criticize their behavior that you will always be there for them no matter what bad thing another individual does. Ensure that you always ask what you can do to help instead of just criticizing what other people do.

- **Heal doubt and overcome trust issues.**

Individuals who have been manipulated by people before find it hard to trust people and are often on the lookout for this type of behavior, so you have to open your eyes to check for signs. If you think that trust is a problem, the fastest way around that issue is to share a private and personal thing with the target. It will be better if they feel you have enough trust in them to share something personal with them or if what you share is relevant to them. It is important that they believe your story and not that it is true. Acting is also key.

When trying to manipulate another individual, doubt is the biggest enemy you will have. They might start to see that they are not behaving like themselves if they notice anything fishy about your behavior. Hopefully, you have learned about their problems and discovered what they desire to change. If they openly question how they are acting, you must tell them that change can be uncomfortable. Still, it is necessary to make progress in their lives.

Negativity should be saved for a necessary emotional outburst. Being positive will always be your best friend when convincing people to do what you desire. Negative manipulation should only be used when necessary, as too much negativity can make you an ineffective manipulator.

What if you're discovered?

If your target starts calling you a manipulator, you should not respond with more manipulative behavior. This is the worst thing you can do. Be a calm and normal person if you are caught. Allow them to assume control of the situation, and don't try to defend yourself. Once caught, the best way to escape the problem is to create doubt in your target's mind.

Create doubt that benefits you. If your target accuses you of being manipulative and you don't react with more manipulation, they may start doubting their thoughts and wonder if they assumed correctly or not. Often, the target will already have an attachment to you and embrace any excuse to believe they have made a wrong assumption about you.

When someone catches you, it is often because another manipulator or their friend has told them something about you. Be careful, be smart, and be prepared to surprise the person if you suddenly get discovered.

Now, what if someone else is trying to manipulate you? How do you recognize that? Let's find out.

Recognizing and Handling Manipulation in Everyday Interactions

Whether at work, in relationships, or even while shopping, manipulation can sneak into our lives. But the good news? With a bit of awareness, you can spot it and steer clear.

Here are examples of how manipulation shows up in everyday situations to help you identify the tactics in various settings and give you concrete ways to respond.

- **At Work**

Example 1:

Situation: You receive an email from a colleague that says, "I guess I'll have to finish the report myself since you didn't have time." This kind of passive-aggressive remark is designed to make you feel guilty.

Response: Address it directly but professionally. You could reply, "I noticed your concern about the report. I'm happy to assist, but I need to understand the timeline better to manage my workload effectively."

Example 2:

Situation: Your boss drops a huge project on your desk at 4 PM on a Friday, saying, "I really need this done by Monday. I know you're the only one who can handle it."

Response: Set boundaries. "I'm committed to delivering high-quality work, but I need adequate time. Can we extend the deadline or reassign some of my current tasks to accommodate this?"

- **In Relationships**

Example 1:

Situation: Your partner gives you the silent treatment because you didn't do something they wanted. This is an emotional manipulation tactic to make you feel anxious and guilty.

Response: Address the behavior directly. "I've noticed you're not speaking to me. Let's discuss what's bothering you so we can resolve it together."

Example 2:

Situation: A friend or partner says, "If you loved me, you'd do this for me," trying to manipulate you into doing something you're uncomfortable with.

Response: Stand your ground. "My feelings for you aren't in question. Let's find a solution that respects both of our needs."

- **In Social Situations**

Example 1:

Situation: A group of friends pressures you to join an activity you're not interested in by saying, "Everyone else is doing it, don't be the odd one out."

Response: Be honest but firm. "I appreciate the invite, but I'm going to sit this one out. Have fun, and let's catch up another time."

Example 2:

Situation: Someone compliments you excessively, then immediately asks for a favor, like, "You're so talented, could you help me with this project?"

Response: Recognize the tactic and decide based on your capacity. "Thank you for the compliment! I'm flattered, but I have a lot on my plate right now."

- **In Consumer Situations**

Example 1:

Situation: A salesperson tells you, "This deal is only available today. You have to act now!" This is to create urgency and pressure you into a quick decision.

Response: Take your time. "I need to think about it. If the deal is good today, it should still be good tomorrow. I'll get back to you."

Example 2:

Situation: A store offers a "free gift" with a purchase, making you feel like you need to buy something so as not to miss out on the gift.

Response: Evaluate the need. "Thank you for the gift offer, but I'll pass on the purchase for now. I'll consider it if I genuinely need the product."

- **Everyday Life**

Example 1:

Situation: A neighbor constantly offers help with small tasks but always expects something in return, like, "I mowed your lawn, so could you watch my pets this weekend?"

Response: Be appreciative but clear about boundaries. "Thanks for mowing the lawn! I'm busy this weekend, so I can't watch your pets. Let's find another way to help each other out."

Example 2:

Situation: A family member says, "You never visit anymore, it's like you don't care about us," to guilt you into spending more time with them.

Response: Express your feelings honestly. "I care about you all a lot. My schedule has been hectic, but I'm trying to balance everything. Let's plan a visit when I can fully enjoy our time together."

Recognizing these manipulation tactics can help you navigate everyday situations more confidently, even if you use them on others.

Story

Here's a story everyone should hear. It explores the insidious nature of dark psychology techniques like gaslighting and manipulation and the importance of emotional intelligence and awareness in recognizing and defending against these tactics. It's a story about a woman named Rachel.

Rachel was the kind of person you immediately liked when you met her. People described her as friendly and hardworking. She was always willing to lend a hand. When Rachel met Harvey at a friend's party, she thought she had finally met her soulmate. He was charming, attentive, and seemed genuinely interested in her life. They started dating, and everything seemed perfect. But then, things began to change...slowly.

It was subtle at first. Harvey would make offhand remarks about Rachel's looks, body, clothes, you name it. When they had a date, he would say things like, "Are you sure you want to wear that?" pretending to be concerned about her appearance. Other times, he'd deny hearing her mention things she had talked to him about, such as an important meeting. These comments seemed insignificant, but Rachel started to doubt herself. Harvey was chipping away at her confidence.

As you know, this is classic gaslighting that makes Rachel doubt her reality. Harvey questions her memory and decisions to gradually make her dependent on his version of reality. Rachel doesn't recognize what is happening at this point.

With time, Harvey's behavior escalated. He started isolating Rachel from her friends and family. "They don't understand our relationship." "They're just jealous." He got upset whenever she spent time with her loved ones, making her feel guilty for "neglecting" him. This was another dark psychology tactic – manipulators isolate their victims to gain more control over them.

Sometimes, when it was necessary, Harvey used covert persuasion to get his way. He would twist their arguments so that Rachel always felt she was wrong. Say she wanted to hang out with friends, he would remind her of a time she asked him to stay home with her – even though it was because of period pains. This made her feel hypocritical. He'd say, "I thought we agreed to spend more time together." His goal was to make her feel selfish for wanting a life outside of their relationship.

Naturally, Rachel felt trapped. She started thinking that perhaps the problem was with her. Her self-esteem took a massive hit, and she found herself constantly trying to avoid conflict with Harvey. She lived in a constant state of anxiety, always second-guessing herself.

Fortunately, Rachel's breakthrough came on a fateful evening. She was scrolling through Quora when she came across a piece about dark psychology techniques, including gaslighting. As she read the article, she could feel a chill running down her spine. It was as if the writer was describing Rachel's relationship with Harvey.

The more Rachel read about manipulation tactics, the more she realized what was happening to her. She felt betrayed and stupid. How could she have been so blind? Rachel reached out to her friend, Emily. Together, they both did more research on dark psychology techniques. They learned specifically about manipulation tactics such as gaslighting and covert persuasion. Rachel realized that Harvey had exploited her kind and trusting nature. She decided enough was enough.

First, Rachel found the strength to leave the relationship. It wasn't easy, but she knew it was necessary for her well-being. Then, determined to make sure nothing like that ever happens to her again, Rachel set out to learn more about dark psychology techniques. She also learned how to protect herself from them. Gradually, she set boundaries and rebuilt her confidence.

Months later, Rachel met someone charming at her local library. This time, she recognized the person's subtle attempts at manipulating her, which enabled her to protect herself and avoid being drawn into another trap.

Rachel's experience with Harvey made her more self-aware and discerning. She even taught her friends how to recognize and protect themselves from manipulation. In the end, while Rachel's trust had been shattered, she became more resilient and slowly rebuilt it.

If you ever find yourself doubting your reality, questioning your worth, or feeling isolated and controlled, take a step back and evaluate your relationship with the person making you feel this way.

Manipulation is just one aspect of dark psychology. Another aspect is deception, which you will learn extensively in the next chapter. Get ready!

CHAPTER FIVE:
The Art Of Deception

In psychology, deception is intentionally or unintentionally misleading people into believing untrue information. It is a common aspect of dark psychology that some people are more skilled at than others. While humans are generally honest, even the most honest individuals engage in deception from time to time.

Research suggests that the average person lies multiple times a day. Some lies are big ("I've never asked that lady out in my life!"), but the prevalent ones are little white lies ("No, you don't look fat in that dress.") to spare feelings or avoid uncomfortable interactions.

Deception is used to take advantage of people's trust in you. Since being truthful is central to humanity, which depends on a shared perception of reality, most people assume that others are forthright in their communications and dealings. So, they tend to instinctively trust what others say – unless they've had a bad experience.

Like any skill, it's possible to master deception through observation, practice, and understanding of human psychology. The skill can be used for varying purposes, benign or exploitative. If you become skilled at it, you can use deception to influence people's thoughts and actions.

The different types of deception include:

- **Lying**: Providing false information intentionally.
- **Omission**: Leaving out important information.
- **Misleading**: Providing information that is technically true but intended to deceive.
- **Exaggeration**: Overstating facts or details.

When done to deceive another person, these actions are considered deceitful. In addition to telling falsehoods, people lie through strategic silence or withhold vital information.

When you think of deception, you might imagine someone fabricating an entire story or false information from scratch. But usually, sheer invention isn't at the heart of deception. Rather, people deceive by agreeing with you when, in fact, they don't. Or they might exaggerate to make themselves look good.

There are different motivations for deception. Some deceive to avoid punishment or negative outcomes, which is a motive of self-protection. Others might deceive for self-enhancement to create a more favorable perception of themselves. Sometimes, people lie to protect others' feelings or for social gains. They also do it to manage interpersonal interactions. Finally, people use deception to achieve specific objectives, such as winning a negotiation or competition.

A good way to think of deception is as a magician's sleight of hand in the middle of an enthralling magic trick. Magicians skillfully distract their audience with one hand while secretly handling objects with others. This is how they create illusions that defy logic and expectation.

Similar to how the magician's speech and gestures divert your attention, people skilled at deception use tactics to distract targets from their true intentions and actions. Just as the magician creates an illusion of magic, these people craft false narratives or perspectives that seem real to deceive others.

The moment a magician reveals the true mechanics of a trick is similar to the shock people feel when they uncover deception. It often leaves them questioning what they once thought was real and true.

Though manipulation and deception are closely linked, they are different things. The former involves influencing or controlling someone else's thoughts, feelings, and actions to serve personal interests. In contrast, deception focuses on creating a false perception or belief in someone else's mind by omitting information, sharing false information, or distorting the truth.

Essentially, deception is a form of manipulation. It is a dark psychology tactic because it can be harmful if used by someone with malicious intentions. Why? Deception exploits trust or reliance on the truth. If used maliciously, it can cause irreparable financial, social, or emotional damage to the target. Also, it operates in stealth mode, which makes it difficult for the target to recognize until damage has been done. This is why deception is an incredibly effective dark psychology technique.

Certain forms of deception, such as harmless pranks or entertainment, are generally benign. They cause no harm. However, deception, as in dark psychology, is mainly used for nefarious reasons, including gaslighting, emotional abuse, and fraud.

Before employing the tactics, know that deception can break trust, damage relationships, and cause long-term psychological harm. It undermines healthy interpersonal dynamics.

Why do you need this skill?

The Psychology of Lying

According to Science Direct, lying is "a form of communication that involves two parties: the deceiver and the deceived." As the deceiver, your goal is to communicate false information or perceptions. However, you need the person on the receiving end to partake in the process on some level. This might be based on bias, ignorance, overconfidence, or learned apathy.

Humans are susceptible for a few reasons. One of these, as mentioned, is the innate tendency to believe others are truthful. Sometimes, this is due to cognitive overwhelm. Other times, it's because emotional displays and arguments convince us.

The psychology of lying is complex, and as bad as it may seem, lying is key to human survival. As we have evolved to more complex social structures, lying has taken a more even intricate role as it has become a powerful tool for acquiring resources.

Individuals skilled in deception may receive a larger share of resources, increasing their chances of survival, reproduction, and promotion. This reality is well observed in evolutionary psychology. It is a universally recognized truth that lying isn't always the best thing. Still, it's the exact thing you need to get ahead sometimes.

Cognitive Aspects of Lying

There are many brain processes involved in lying. Understanding these is fundamental to mastering the art of deception. Unlike the truth, a lie is more mentally demanding, requiring many cognitive functions.

When you lie, the brain has to:

- **Inhibit the truth**. Your brain knows the truth, even if the person you are lying to doesn't. Because the truth is more readily accessible, the brain has to work overtime to suppress it. This takes a lot of mental effort, increasing the cognitive load.
- **Create the lie**. If you're fabricating an entirely false narrative, the brain must generate information that has never been processed. This requires creativity, which, of course, increases the cognitive load.
- **Maintain consistency**. Once you tell a lie, you must remember it and ensure it correlates with future statements. Your brain needs substantial mental resources, especially if you've said multiple lies or a single, complex lie.
- **Process dual tasks**. As you're telling a lie, your brain must simultaneously manage the fabricated and real narrative. This

further increases cognitive load and the possibility of making an error.

To lie effectively, you must possess the ability to attribute mental states to yourself and the other person. You should know what they will accept or believe to develop a plausible lie. Also, lying instigates a dissonance between your beliefs and actions. You must devise justifications for your lies to address the discomfort from the cognitive dissonance.

Different brain regions are engaged in the cognitive aspects of lying:

- **Prefrontal Cortex**: This area is crucial for decision-making, problem-solving, and social behavior. It helps in planning the lie and controlling truthful responses.
- **Anterior Cingulate Cortex (ACC):** The ACC is involved in error detection and conflict monitoring. It becomes active when managing the internal conflict of lying.
- **Amygdala**: This region processes emotions like fear and anxiety, which are often associated with lying. Increased activity in the amygdala can indicate the emotional stress of lying.

Anatomy of a Lie

The anatomy of a lie involves several key components that work together to create a falsehood. Here's a breakdown of these components:

1. **Intention**: Every lie starts with an intention. This is the decision to deceive someone. You need a reason for lying, whether it's to protect yourself, gain something, or avoid consequences.
2. **Construction**: Next, you construct the lie. This involves coming up with a plausible story that fits the situation. The details must be consistent and believable to avoid suspicion.

3. **Delivery**: The way the lie is delivered is crucial. Nonverbal signals such as body language, facial expressions, and tone of voice must align with the spoken words to make the lie convincing. Any inconsistency can give the lie away.
4. **Maintenance**: Once the lie is told, it needs to be maintained. This can involve remembering the details, reinforcing the lie with additional falsehoods if questioned, and keeping the story straight over time.
5. **Preventing Detection**: Lies can be detected through various means, such as inconsistencies in the story, changes in behavior, or evidence that contradicts the lie. Skilled liars often anticipate this and take steps to minimize the chances of detection.
6. **Consequences**: Every lie has potential consequences. If the lie is discovered, it can lead to loss of trust, damaged relationships, and other negative outcomes. You must weigh these risks against the perceived benefits of lying.

Understanding these components can help you create more plausible lies and recognize when someone attempts to deceive you, whether in personal relationships, professional settings, or other areas of life.

Common Deception Techniques

The most effective deception techniques use either falsification or concealment. In concealment, you withhold some of the information without telling an outright lie. In falsification, you take an additional step. You don't just withhold the truth; you also present false/fabricated information as if it were true. Often, the best lies combine both approaches. However, skilled liars usually get away with just concealment.

Many don't even consider concealment a lie; they use that word in cases of complete falsification. If a doctor doesn't tell his patient the illness is terminal, that's concealment. But even if no false information was shared, it's still a form of deception – as long as the target has been misled in any form.

Here are the most common and effective deception techniques based on concealment or falsification.

1. **Omission**

This technique involves leaving out important information that could change your target's understanding or perception of the situation. The omission of key details creates a misleading impression without you needing to share a false statement outright. For example, you might tell your partner you went for lunch with friends without mentioning that you saw and caught up with your ex at the restaurant.

Omission is incredibly effective since it rarely gets noticed. The target often doesn't realize critical information is missing, so they can't confront you.

2. **Misdirection**

This technique is used to divert attention away from the truth or issue. You might change the subject, focus on something else, or introduce irrelevant details. Misdirection is best applied when the other person is easily distracted or you're in control of the narrative. For instance, someone confronted about missing funds might start talking about a recent charity event they donated to misdirect the confronter.

If done skillfully, your target may forget their original question or concern. This increases your chances of avoiding detection.

3. **Minimization**

Sometimes, the best way to deceive another person is to downplay the significance or severity of a fact, an action, or an event. It makes a lie appear more reasonable and believable by reducing the impact. For instance, you might describe a significant mistake at work as "just a small oversight" to avoid blame. The person you tell the lie to may ignore the need to react strongly or probe further, which makes it easier to maintain the lie.

4. Exaggeration

Exaggeration involves making something more significant or dramatic than necessary. You might make a situation, action, or fact seem more important or larger than it is. It's a great technique for manipulating perceptions and reactions. For example, you might claim you worked 80 hours a week on a work project to impress your boss when you worked 50.

This technique utilizes the human tendency to react strongly to extremes. If an exaggeration aligns with your target's desires or expectations, they may accept it unquestioningly.

5. Fabrication

Sometimes, you can deceive by creating entirely false information or narratives. This is an outright lie that requires conception and consistency. For instance, someone might lie about having a prestigious degree from a top university to gain credibility. This technique is tricky because the lie requires plenty of details and consistency. But there's a risk of detection with further investigation.

6. Denial

This is when you refuse to acknowledge the truth or existence of something. You have to reject whatever allegations or facts you're presented with. Denial works best in situations with a lack of conclusive evidence. For example, an employee caught slacking off might deny ever doing so. The firmer and more consistent you are, the more doubt you will instill in people's minds. Ultimately, this makes it harder to prove the lie.

7. Feigning Ignorance

Here, you pretend to be unaware or uninformed about something to evade suspicion or responsibility. For instance, if asked about a missing document, you might claim you have no idea where it is, even though you've hidden it.

Feigning ignorance works because ignorance calls less attention than deception. People find it easier to believe someone doesn't know something than to suspect them of lying.

How to Tell an Undetectable Lie

Telling an undetectable lie is an art. Understanding the mechanics can be super insightful. So, here's a step-by-step guide on how to make your lies harder to detect.

Stick close to the truth.

The best lies are those close to the truth. If you base a lie on a real event or experience, the brain doesn't have to do too much to remember it. This makes it harder to detect or disprove. So, when crafting a lie, change one or two details about a true situation.

Example:

- **Truth**: You went to a café last weekend.
- **Lie**: You tell your friend you saw an old acquaintance at the café.
- **Why It Works**: The main part of the story (going to the café) is true, so you can recall genuine details about the visit, making the lie about seeing an acquaintance more believable.

Keep it simple.

Simple lies are easier to remember and reduce the chances of being caught in contradictions. The more complex a lie is, the harder it is to remember and the greater your inconsistencies. So, when crafting your lie, focus on a few key points instead of adding too many details that can be questioned.

Example:

- **Complex Lie**: "I spent the entire weekend at my cousin's house. We went hiking, then to a concert, and met some famous people backstage."
- **Simple Lie**: "I spent the weekend at my cousin's house."
- **Why It Works**: The simpler lie is less likely to be questioned and easier to maintain under scrutiny.

Practice your story.

Rehearsing your lie ensures you can tell it smoothly and confidently without hesitation, which is key to believability. Go over your lie multiple times until you can deliver it smoothly and without hesitation. You can practice in front of a mirror or with a trusted friend (if the lie isn't about them) to see how convincing you are.

Example:

- **Practice**: If you're lying about why you were late, practice saying, "There was a heavy traffic jam on the highway due to an accident, and it took forever to clear."
- **Why It Works**: Rehearsing helps you deliver the lie naturally and without stumbling, which can raise suspicion.

Match your nonverbal cues with the lie.

Nonverbal cues can indicate a lie. Keeping your body language and tone of voice natural helps maintain the illusion of truth. Avoid fidgeting, excessive blinking, or other nervous habits that indicate deception. Also, keep a steady voice; too much variation can be a giveaway.

Example:

- **Lie**: "I really enjoyed the presentation."
- **Body Language**: Smile slightly, make eye contact, and nod.
- **Why It Works**: Consistent body language and a steady tone match the words, making the lie more believable.

Control your emotions.

Keep your emotions in check. Overreacting or underreacting can raise suspicion. Deliver your lie with confidence. Hesitation can be a red flag.

Example:

- **Scenario**: You're lying about not being upset about missing an event.
- **Lie**: "It's no big deal, I'll catch the next one."
- **Why It Works**: If you show genuine calmness and lack of emotion, your actions will align with your words and make the lie seem true.

Anticipate questions.

Consider what questions might arise and prepare answers that are consistent with your lie. Make sure any additional details align with your main story.

Example:

- **Lie**: "I couldn't come to the party because I was feeling sick."
- **Anticipated Question**: "What were your symptoms?"
- **Prepared Answer**: "I had a terrible headache and felt nauseous all day."
- **Why It Works**: Being ready with consistent details prevents you from getting caught off guard.

Monitor the other person's reactions.

It's important to pay attention to the listener's reactions and be ready to adjust your story if needed. If you sense disbelief, subtly shift your story to address concerns without making it obvious.

Example:

- **Lie**: "I saw Sarah at the store yesterday."
- **Reaction**: The listener looks skeptical.
- **Adjustment**: "Maybe it wasn't her, I was in a hurry and didn't get a good look."

- * Why It Works: Quickly adapting to the listener's reaction can defuse suspicion.

End the conversation gracefully.

Wrapping up the conversation smoothly can prevent further questioning and scrutiny. Change the subject to divert attention away from the lie.

Example:

- **Lie**: "I've already finished that report."
- **End**: "Anyway, I've got to get to my next meeting. Talk later?"
- **Why It Works**: Ending the conversation shifts focus away from the lie and reduces the chance of it being probed further.

You must know when to lie and when not to lie. If the risks outweigh the benefits, you shouldn't deceive the person, especially if there may be severe consequences or it may damage your relationship forever.

The bottom line is that an undetectable lie combines elements of the truth with simplicity, adaptability, controlled emotions and nonverbal cues, and preparation.

To be a true master of the art of detection, you must also be able to tell when others are lying to you.

Detecting Lies: Tools and Tips

Can you tell when a person is lying to you? Most people believe they can, but the evidence suggests otherwise. We aren't as good at spotting lies as we like to think. Research indicates that detecting a lie depends more on how bad the lie is than how good the other person is at detecting it.

Lying is a common human behavior, so you'll probably have people trying to deceive you at every point in life. Now, there's no surefire way to discover when another person is being deceptive. However, there are possible red flags that can serve as indicators, such as:

- Offering vague or few details
- Repeating the story over and over
- Repeating your questions before answering them
- Using sentence fragments in spoken communication Explaining the story in a strict chronological order
- Sounding like the story is rehearsed
- Failing to offer specific details when challenged
- Being unable to provide straightforward answers to simple yes or no questions
- Physical changes, such as fidgeting, sweating, tensed muscles, etc
- Fiddling with hair or pressing fingers to lips

These cues may indicate when someone is lying, but they aren't conclusive proof of deception. Someone anxious for another reason may display some of the signs.

If you suspect someone isn't being truthful, examine the following indicators to determine whether their story is fact or fiction.

Body Language

Body language cues are some of your best bets for lie detection. People's body language often betray their words or intentions. I mean subtle behavioral and physical "tells" that reveal deception. For instance, a bored posture, shrugging, and lack of facial expression can give away someone who might be deceptive.

Someone lying may display nervous habits like touching their face, avoiding eye contact, or fidgeting. However, some highly skilled liars know how to do the opposite to maintain an appearance of honesty. Watch out for inconsistencies between their words and body language.

Example: Picture a scenario where a friend is telling you a story about how they spent their weekend. They say they were at a quiet retreat but can't sit still and keep looking away. Their body language might indicate they did something different.

Tone of Voice

Changes in a person's vocal pitch or speech patterns may be signs of deception. For example, they might suddenly start speaking slower or faster or have visible changes in their tone. Another indicator is if they clear their throat consecutively.

Example: A coworker's voice starts to quiver during a conversation, or they start speaking in a higher pitch out of the blue. This could be a sign of feeling uncomfortable with what they are saying.

Microexpressions

As you know, microexpressions reveal a person's true emotions. They are split-second facial movements that are incredibly hard to fake. Thus, they can be quite telling, especially if they don't match the words coming out of a person's mouth.

Example: If someone claims to be happy for you over a promotion but you notice a quick flash of sadness or jealousy, that's their true feelings slipping through.

Details

A liar will often trip on details when telling a fabricated story. They might find it hard to keep their face straight. You can challenge them with specific questions to see if the story holds up. Inconsistency is a sign of deception.

Example: A coworker apologizes for being late to work because they were stuck in traffic. Ask about the route they took. They could be lying to you if they can't provide an immediate answer.

Timing and Duration

Timing is crucial in lie detection. If someone pauses before they answer your question, they might be coming up with a lie. Also, if their story is too detailed, they might try too hard to seem truthful.

Example: When you ask your boyfriend a straightforward question, like where they were last night, and they take too long to respond or give an elaborate answer, be careful. That could be a lie.

Baselining

Imagine you're trying to determine if someone is being truthful or not. But you can't conclude based on a fleeting facial expression or gesture. That's where baselining comes in. Think of it as setting the other person's normal behavior benchmark.

When you start talking to someone, you must first pay attention to their physical behavior when relaxed and having a normal conversation. Notice their body language, facial expressions, tone of voice, speech patterns, etc. Do they fidget with their hands or feet? Do they have a particular rhythm in their speech?

This is called establishing a baseline. It gives you a sense of your target's normal behavior. Once there's a baseline, you can compare it to their behavior when you suspect they're deceptive or hiding something. If there is a significant deviation from the baseline – such as suddenly avoiding eye contact or displaying unusual body language – that could mean deception.

However, remember that deviations aren't necessarily foolproof signals of deception. They indicate something is off with the person, and you must probe further. Humans react differently to discomfort, anxiety, and other factors unrelated to lying.

The purpose of baselining in lie detection is to help you avoid false positives. It's easy to misrepresent stress or anxiety as dishonesty without a baseline. But when you know what normal behavior is, you can easily spot when a person acts out of character.

Whether you want to become a human lie detector or sharpen your deception skills, these tips and strategies should help.

Story

Let me tell you a story about Bill.

Bill was the kind of guy who could sell ice to an Eskimo. He had a knack for telling stories that captivated his audience, and people often believed him without a second thought. His friends used to joke that Bill could convince you the sky was green if he wanted to.

One day, Bill's skills were tested at a poker game. His circle knew him as an expert bluffer, but this game was different. A new player, Will, had joined and was reputed to be a human lie detector. The stakes were high, and the tension in the room was palpable.

As the game progressed, Bill found himself in a tight spot. He had a mediocre hand but needed to bluff his way through to win the pot. He maintained his usual calm demeanor, casually chatting and making jokes, all while keeping a close eye on Will.

Bill knew the importance of baselining. Throughout the night, he studied Will's behavior – how he reacted to different hands, his facial expressions, and his tone of voice. Bill had a mental catalog of Will's tells when he was confident and bluffing.

When the crucial moment came, Bill made his move. He bet big, pushing a stack of chips into the center of the table. The room fell silent, and all eyes were on Will. Would he call Bill's bluff?

Will stared at Bill, trying to read him. Bill stayed cool, his face a mask of calm confidence. Will looked for any deviation from Bill's baseline behavior, but there was none. Bill's poker face was perfect.

After what felt like an eternity, Will sighed and folded his cards. Bill released a breath he didn't realize he was holding and revealed his mediocre hand. The table erupted in laughter and groans. Bill had done it again – he had bluffed his way to victory.

After the game, Will approached Bill, a grin on his face. "You're good," he said, shaking his head. "I couldn't read you at all."

Bill smiled. "It's all about knowing the baseline," he said. "And never letting them see you sweat."

Bill's mastery of lying and detecting lies was a combination of his natural talent and his keen observation skills. He understood that the key to both was baselining – knowing what was normal to spot what wasn't. And that night, it made all the difference.

CHAPTER SIX:

Hypnosis: Unlocking The Subconscious

Hypnosis is a trance-like state of focused attention and heightened suggestibility. When hypnotized, you can become more open to suggestions, which might help you change certain behaviors, perceptions, or feelings. It's often used for therapeutic purposes, such as assisting people to quit smoking, reduce stress, or manage pain.

During hypnosis, a trained therapist or hypnotist uses verbal prompts and imagery to guide you into this state. You're not asleep or unconscious; you're usually aware of what's happening but feel deeply relaxed.

Hypnosis can be used for manipulation, but it's not as simple as often portrayed in movies or TV shows. Hypnosis relies heavily on the willingness and cooperation of the person being hypnotized. You can't hypnotize people against their will or make them do something that goes against their morals or beliefs.

The idea that someone else can cause you to do something you would ordinarily not do can be scary. So, it is not surprising that many individuals choose to doubt the effects of hypnosis. Although some individuals may not agree that hypnosis is real, nothing can change the fact that it is real. In our modern world today, hypnotherapy has been used for treating a variety of conditions, including skin conditions and pain.

Many people dismiss hypnosis as medically unfounded, but David Spiegel, MD, who is an expert in clinical hypnosis, has published years of research studying the influence of hypnosis on brain activity and how effective it is in controlling pain related to fibromyalgia, cancer, and surgery.

Hypnosis can change the brain's perception of pain. Individuals experiencing pain often use hypnosis when they have tried everything to stop the pain and failed. But Spiegel says hypnosis should be the first thing to do.

Spiegel also uses hypnosis on himself. He had a recurrent dislocated shoulder and had surgery at Massachusetts General Hospital. Afterwards, he used self-hypnosis for pain control.

Some individuals are not as susceptible to hypnosis as others. When an individual is under hypnosis, the hypnotist guides the individual's actions. Still, the individual is not disoriented, as movies might make you believe. People react in different ways when hypnotized and are not as sleepy and helpless as the movies make them seem.

It might be not easy to believe that hypnosis can control someone's mind. You might have seen hypnosis in magic shows, where the magician hypnotizes someone, and the person does some things they would not do in their right state of mind. When the magician snaps them out of that state, they have no idea what happened during that short period.

Note that hypnosis isn't magic or mind control. It's a legitimate technique recognized by medical and psychological professionals.

So, do you want to hypnotize someone but are unsure how? How can you successfully hypnotize someone? I'll show you, but first, let's discuss common myths and facts about hypnosis.

Understanding Hypnosis: Myths and Facts

There are quite a few misconceptions about hypnosis. Let's break down some common myths and the corresponding facts:

Myth 1: Hypnosis is mind control or brainwashing.

Fact: Hypnosis cannot make you do something against your will. While under hypnosis, you remain fully aware of your actions and can reject any suggestion against your morals or beliefs.

Myth 2: You might get stuck in hypnosis and never wake up.

Fact: It's impossible to get stuck in hypnosis. You can come out of the hypnotic state at any time, either on your own or when the hypnotist guides you back to full awareness.

Myth 3: Only those with weak minds can be hypnotized.

Fact: Hypnosis has nothing to do with the strength of your mind. It's about your willingness and ability to follow the hypnotist's suggestions. People who can concentrate well and have a strong imagination are often more easily hypnotized.

Myth 4: Hypnosis is just a trick used in stage shows.

Fact: While stage hypnosis is real, it's performed for entertainment and differs from therapeutic hypnosis. Clinical hypnosis is a legitimate therapeutic tool used by trained professionals to help with various conditions like anxiety, pain, and smoking cessation.

Myth 5: Hypnosis can make you reveal your deepest secrets.

Fact: You have control over what you say and do during hypnosis. You won't reveal any secrets unless you want to. Hypnosis cannot compel you to share anything you wouldn't normally share.

Myth 6: Hypnosis is dangerous.

Fact: Hypnosis is generally safe when conducted by a trained professional. It represents a natural state of focused attention and relaxation with minimal risks. However, it is important to ensure that the hypnotist is certified and experienced.

Myth 7: You're unconscious or asleep during hypnosis.

Fact: Hypnosis is a state of heightened awareness and focus. You're not asleep or unconscious and are usually aware of what's happening around you, although you may feel deeply relaxed.

Myth 8: Hypnosis can cure any ailment.

Fact: While hypnosis can be effective for managing certain conditions like pain, stress, and anxiety, it's not a cure-all. It's often used as a complementary treatment alongside other medical or psychological therapies.

Myth 9: Hypnosis can enhance memory recall.

Fact: Hypnosis can sometimes help improve focus and concentration, but it doesn't necessarily enhance memory. It can sometimes result in the formation of false memories, which is why it's used cautiously in legal settings.

Understanding the realities of hypnosis is key to using it appropriately.

Now, how do you use hypnosis?

Techniques of Hypnosis

Practical Applications of Hypnosis

Hypnotizing someone isn't just about clicking your fingers and asking someone to sleep. There is a lot you need to understand. As previously explained, hypnosis is not just a trick of showmen and magicians; it has practical applications in therapy and pain management. For instance, it is used in the treatment of addictions, overcoming psychological fears, and reducing pain for burn victims and patients with severe injuries. Some people even use it to lose weight and ease labor pains during childbirth.

When practicing hypnosis, it's important to choose someone who would be open to your suggestions.

Choosing the Right Person

You have a desire, and you need someone to fulfill it. So, you have to find someone fitting. You can't hypnotize someone who doesn't want to be hypnotized. Say an individual isn't open to it. When you try to hypnotize them, they will likely not go into that state of heightened suggestibility.

After finding the person to hypnotize, you need to ensure that they are the right individuals to hypnotize and that you can safely practice with them. Some individuals are not as safe as others when hypnosis is involved, and some others should not undergo the process at all.

Ensure that the individual you have chosen to hypnotize doesn’t have personality disorders, dementia, psychosis, psychological disorders, brain trauma, uncontrolled epilepsy/seizures, severe clinical depression, or severe cognitive deficits/learning difficulties.

Setting the Stage

Once you have someone you want to hypnotize, you must find a location to use. You must have heard that a completely silent and comfortable environment is necessary for hypnosis to be successful. You need to find a place to avoid interruptions when starting. You must set up for success by ensuring comfort and fewer distractions.

Preparing for Hypnosis

Once you are with the person you want to hypnotize, you can start by doing a pre-talk. This will help them relax and ensure they are comfortable before you start. An individual who is not relaxed or has other things on their mind will probably not go into hypnosis. You can begin the pre-talk by asking them about their thoughts and any concerns they may have. It will also be helpful to ask about their previous experience as it can positively or negatively affect the hypnosis.

The Process of Hypnosis

You can try progressive relaxation induction since it's the most common method of inducing a state of hypnosis. In this method, you give the individual "suggestions" to help them progressively relax their mind and body. This can take only a few minutes, not hours. Before the hypnosis begins, consider how you will deliver the relaxing suggestions. Your voice should portray relaxation and convey confidence. Ensure that your voice sounds relaxing and confident when you are ready to start with your hypnotic suggestions.

You can begin by asking the individual to take three deep breaths and then proceed to ask them to close their eyes. Once the person has closed their eyes, direct suggestions can continue, including calming their mind, breathing slowly, and relaxing their body as your voice makes them feel comfortable. Repetition is important. You can use similar suggestions repeatedly and vary them slightly sometimes. Suggest that the individual relaxes their muscles, beginning at their feet and moving up through their entire body. Next, suggest that they imagine themselves going down a staircase of 15 steps, each making them feel more relaxed.

Give the individual enough time to listen and comply with your suggestions. Even though you may feel like rushing through the suggestions, take it slowly and give them enough time to respond. You are trying to make them feel relaxed, so you must also feel comfortable.

During Hypnosis

After getting the person to relax, the individual should be trance-like. Some individuals remain light throughout the process, while others go deep into hypnosis. Once the person is hypnotized, you can then do what you want. They will respond to the suggestions you give, whether they are for entertainment or therapy. Individuals who are deeply hypnotized and responsive may be able to easily respond to hypnotic suggestions and engage in more complex therapy techniques under your direction.

Ending the Hypnosis

It is easy to wake the individual from hypnosis. You only need to tell them that you will count from 1 to 5, and then they will wake up. You can suggest that they become more alert, awake, and energized. Ensure you provide the individual with suggestions to make them feel good when they wake up.

Now, you're probably wondering how possible it is to use hypnosis techniques to achieve your goals and desires in your daily life. For instance, can you convince your child to stay focused on their studies, make someone fall in love with you, or make your boss allow you to leave work early every day? Well, the most skilled hypnotists can achieve different things in life through mind control.

To some extent, we are already subject to a form of hypnosis daily without realizing it. This may even happen to you when you like someone and follow them. For example, if you notice that you follow your friend to go out for dinner or a movie without thinking about it when you are meant to stay at home and study for an exam, that's like being under hypnosis. They only need to suggest it for you to come along.

If a person likes you, they may do whatever you want to make you happy. Thus, you may have said yes to something you don't want to do simply because you are attracted to the person asking you to do that favor or you like the person.

But what if the person is a stranger, like a prospective client or a salesperson? In this case, you must use the hypnosis technique of mirroring their behavior and body language. Watch the individual carefully and pick up some repetitive words or actions that they use. Ensure that you use the same actions or words during your interactions with that individual, and they will see your similarities with them, which will help develop a rapport.

Controlling People Through Stories

Have you noticed that individuals get engrossed when watching movies or reading an interesting story and try to copy the character that most impacted their minds? So, while conversing with people daily, include some short anecdotes that will make it possible to control the other person's mind. Negative sentences can even help you make someone do what you want them to do. Reverse psychology is like this. You tell the individual that they don't need to do a particular thing right now. Then they go ahead and do that thing immediately. And this is actually what you want them to do.

When asking people to do something, ensure that you choose your words carefully, as individuals often imagine an image of what you said they should do. When you tell someone they should not allow the glass cup to drop, the person imagines it falling and may even imagine themselves making it fall. But if you ask them to transport it safely, chances are that they will do their best to transport it carefully.

You can try these techniques in your everyday life. You can learn hypnotism and improve over time with practice. You must know how to make an individual come out of a trance when you make them go under a trance. They should come out of the trance without any negative consequences. Some hypnotics use a word, click, or clap to make an individual come out of a deep sleep or undergo a trance. You are using hypnosis to make the subconscious mind more alert than the conscious mind.

You have no idea what the individual has stored in their subconscious mind that may also harm them and you. So, ensure that you are careful when you are trying the techniques. You can try mind control techniques that are easier every day and make your partner return home early or get a good bargain for a product from a salesperson. Ensure the attractive man or woman sitting opposite you in the bar doesn't hypnotize you.

Achieving Your Goals with Self-Hypnosis

People often use self-hypnosis to modify emotions, behavior, and attitudes. For example, many individuals deal with the daily problems of life with self-hypnosis. Self-hypnosis can help develop new skills and boost confidence. It helps relieve anxiety and stress and is also useful for overcoming habits such as overeating and smoking.

Sportsmen and women can use self-hypnosis to enhance their athletic performance, and hypnosis is also useful for individuals suffering from stress-related illnesses or physical pain. Before hypnosis can be used for stress-related illnesses or physical pain, a medical diagnosis has to be made, and it has to be under a qualified therapist or doctor's guidance.

When you hypnotize someone else, that is hetero hypnosis. It is officially known as hypnotherapy. However, self-induced hypnosis is known as autohypnosis or self-hypnosis.

Technique for Self-hypnosis

Let us take a look at an effective self-hypnosis technique. This simple technique is effective and popular, and it is known as eye fixation self-hypnosis. It can help you relax. We will first use it for relaxation and then add hypnotic suggestions and imagery. Start by entering a room where you will not be distracted and then turning off your computer, television, or phone. This will help you reduce distractions. This time is yours, and you will be focusing on nothing else but your goal of self-hypnosis.

Do the following:

1. Sit in a comfortable chair, and don't cross your legs and feet. Ensure that you don't eat a large meal just before you start hypnosis to avoid feeling uncomfortable or bloated. Avoid lying on a bed, as it will likely make you fall asleep. Sit in a comfortable chair so that you don't nod off. Removing your shoes and wearing clothing that is not too tight is best. It is also advisable to remove any contact lenses if you wear them. Avoid crossing your legs and feet.
2. Fix your gaze on the ceiling and breathe deeply. Without tilting your neck to the back or straining your neck, look for a spot on

the ceiling and keep your eyes on that spot. While you fix your gaze on that spot, take a deep breath and breathe. Ensure that you hold it for a moment before breathing out. Silently say the suggestion, "I want to sleep now, my eyes are heavy." Continue repeating this process, and let your eyes close and relax. When you say the suggestion, say it as if you mean it. You can tell it convincingly and soothingly.

3. Allow your body to relax. Free yourself and allow your body to become loose. The next thing to do is slowly count from ten to zero. Tell yourself that you are getting more relaxed with every count. Focus on your breathing while you remain in this relaxed state for some minutes. Be aware of how your diaphragm and chest are rising and falling. Pay attention to how your body is becoming relaxed without you doing too much to relax it. Your body becomes more comfortable the less you try to calm it.
4. Use visualization. Visualize an image that stands for something you desire mastery of and see yourself accomplishing your goal. Say a positive suggestion related to the goal, such as "I am calm, confident, and relaxed," three times. Say it to yourself with conviction while visualizing the image of what you desire for about one minute. Repeat this suggestion three times, and ensure you stay hypnotic between times. Also, be focused on relaxing your body.
5. Return to the room when you are ready by counting from one to ten. Let yourself know that you are becoming aware of your surroundings, and you will open your eyes at the count of ten. Start counting up from one to ten energetically. When you reach ten, you can open your eyes and stretch your legs and arms. Practice the technique up to four or five times, and pay attention to how you become deeply relaxed each time.

If you try this technique and discover it doesn't make you feel as relaxed as you would like, don't give up or force it. You only need to continue practicing regularly to become better at it. Sometimes, individuals will feel drowsy after hypnosis. This is harmless and only takes a few seconds. It is similar to how you feel when you wake up from an afternoon nap. Although this is harmless, ensure you do not operate machinery or drive until fully awake.

More tips…

Have you ever tried to remember a name and found yourself frustrated because you couldn’t remember it? The more you try to remember it, the harder it becomes. Then the name comes back to you later when you are relaxed. Sometimes, we block ourselves from accomplishing our goals when we try too hard.

Your attitude toward self-hypnosis will determine whether you get better at it or not. Relax, and don't set unrealistic goals. Set realistic goals and take your time. You may not achieve results as fast as you want, but you should accept the pace at which things are going, even though the results may initially seem small. Stop doubting yourself and believe you can do it. With time, you will accomplish your goal.

As the years pass by, hypnotherapists have created suggestion rules. The rules have been summarized below. They will help you achieve success with self-hypnosis or hypnotizing someone else.

- **Suggestions should be in the present tense and should be phrased positively.**

Many people will not react more favorably to a negatively worded suggestion as much as they would respond to a positively worded one. You will have more effective suggestions when you talk about what you want to move toward and not what you want to get away from. For instance, instead of saying, "I am not scared," you can say, "I am calm."

Would you rather hear something like, “Would you mind doing this?” or “Do not say you won’t do this.”

It is better to say, "I stop drinking alcohol with ease" instead of "I will try to stop drinking alcohol" because using the word try means that you are struggling to stop drinking alcohol and finding it hard to stop. Your suggestions should be phrased as though they were taking place presently. They should be in the present tense.

So, it is better to say, "I am relaxed in the car" instead of "I will be relaxed when I am in the car." Or you can say, "My confidence is increasing," instead of "I will try my best to be confident."

- **Say the suggestions as if you mean what you are saying.**

How do actors perform? Have you ever seen any of them speaking quietly and mumbling their lines on stage? The performance will not be convincing. People often repeat hypnotic suggestions silently. It is not like acting. However, when repeating the suggestions, you need to say the suggestions as if you mean what you are saying. Be confident, positive, and reassuring.

- **Repetition is important**

Advertisers value suggestions, so they regularly repeat radio and television commercials. Repetition is an important rule when an individual is practicing self-hypnosis. It helps drive the point home and create positive change.

- **Your suggestions should be realistic and specific.**

You will have more effective suggestions if they are realistic and specific. Suppose you have the desire to improve your basketball performance. In that case, you cannot unrealistically give the suggestion, "I am a world-class basketball player," unless you are truly a world champion or are about to become one. Instead, find out what specific thing you wish to improve regarding how you play basketball.

Say you desire to improve a specific area of your basketball playing. You should give realistic suggestions that are specific to that part. Your suggestions should be structured based on the changes you can make that are within your control and not unrealistic things, such as external events, that are not within your control. Do not give suggestions for more than one issue at once.

For example, when you use the suggestion, "I am confident that I can stop smoking and lose weight," you will notice that it is not effective. Instead, pick one goal at a time and work on it, repeating suggestions related to that goal. After you see results, move ahead to the next goal you have.

Follow the above rules, and you should be successful in your hypnosis attempts.

Story

It's natural to be curious about hypnosis, especially after seeing how it's portrayed in movies and TV shows. This was certainly the case for Emma, whose story might make you think twice before volunteering to be hypnotized.

Emma was fascinated by the idea that someone else could reach into the depths of her mind and reveal secrets or even help break her nasty smoking habit. She decided to give hypnosis a try but never figured out how to go about it. That was until a neighbor invited her to a small gathering. This was when Emma saw the dark side of hypnosis.

The gathering at Emma's neighbor's house was a casual evening with a mix of people she recognized and those she didn't. Among the new faces was Dr. Stevan, who was a professional hypnotist. The doctor was charming and articulate. He effortlessly drew everyone into conversations about the power of the mind. Before long, he suggested a hypnosis demonstration. Emma was elated and intrigued. She enthusiastically volunteered for it.

Dr. Stevan had her sit in a comfortable chair and spoke slowly and soothingly. The entire room was silent as he guided Emma into a deep relaxation. She focused on his voice, feeling her mind drift. It felt like she was floating, and soon, Emma was trance-like. He asked her to recall a happy memory, and she did. Everyone was mesmerized as they watched her, eyes closed, responding to his suggestions. It seemed harmless – until things took a different turn.

The doctor started probing deeper, asking about Emma's fears and secrets. He began with the minor stuff—such as her fear of spiders and little childhood embarrassments—but then he started asking about her deepest fears and regrets. Emma felt an uncomfortable tug at her subconscious but couldn't resist his suggestions. Words spilled out, things she hadn't even admitted to herself.

When he finally brought her out of the trance, Emma felt vulnerable and disoriented. Everyone was laughing, talking about how amazing the doctor's skills were. But for her, it was different. She felt exposed – Dr. Stevan had laid bare her innermost thoughts. Over the next couple of days, she couldn't shake the feeling of unease.

She started having vivid dreams and unsettling thoughts. It was as if the hypnosis had opened a door in her mind that she couldn't close. Worse, she noticed changes in my behavior. She was more irritable, anxious, and had trouble focusing.

Emma reached out to Dr. Stevan, wanting him to help. He assured her the aftereffects were normal and would pass within a few more days. But they didn't. Instead, they worsened. She felt like her mind had been manipulated in ways beyond her control, and the thought terrified her.

So, she set out on research and discovered the dark side of hypnosis. Though it can be harmless and even beneficial, hypnosis is also quite dangerous. It can lead to significant consequences if not conducted responsibly.

As you know, hypnosis taps into the subconscious, making the subject highly suggestible. In cases of irresponsibility, hypnosis can uncover traumatic memories or plant false ones. This often leads to confusion and distress. Some people even experience post-hypnotic suggestions that influence their behavior without them realizing it.

Desperate for help, Emma sought the help of a therapist who could help her regain control over her thoughts and emotions. The process was long and slow, but the fog lifted eventually, and she felt like herself again.

Emma discovered that Stevan wasn't a licensed hypnotherapist a few months later. Reflecting on the experience, she realized she was naive to trust an unknown person with such power over her mind.

Hypnosis can be a powerful tool, but it's not without risks. It's essential to know the credentials and ethics of the hypnotist. More importantly, understand that your mind is your most private sanctuary. Not everyone should have access to it. So, if you're ever tempted to try hypnosis, think carefully. Ask yourself: do you want someone else to have that level of control over you?

The dark side of hypnosis is real, and it's not something to take lightly. Emma learned that the hard way.

If hypnosis seems too unrealistic for you, NLP is another dark psychology technique for changing people's minds or behavior. What is NLP? How can you start using it in your daily interactions?

Let's find out in the next chapter.

CHAPTER SEVEN:
Neuro-Linguistics Programming: Rewiring The Mind

Many people are fascinated by techniques that can influence others' thoughts. Imagine entering someone's dream and learning their secrets or planting ideas. If you could do this, you'd change someone's mind from within, making them believe the idea was theirs.

You might think, "I can't enter people's dreams." But you can still plant ideas in people's minds without doing that. The key is Neuro-Linguistic Programming (NLP). I know you're wondering what NLP is and how it can help you control people's minds.

Neuro-linguistic programming, also known as NLP, is a psychology-based approach that involves analyzing people's thoughts, language, and patterns of behavior and applying them to achieve a specific outcome. It was developed in the 1970s by Richard Bandler and John Grinder.

The purpose of NLP is to help people understand how they organize their thoughts, emotions, language, and behavior. It is based on the idea that our perception of the world influences how we operate in day-to-day life. Changing your thoughts can change your life, which sounds simple enough. NLP techniques often include visualization, anchoring (associating a feeling or behavior with a physical stimulus), and modeling (copying others' behaviors).

Some people argue that NLP can be used for mind control, but it's not so much that as it is influence and persuasion. Yes, it is possible to use NLP techniques to get people to think or act in certain ways – without their conscious awareness.

Imagine if you had the NLP skills to plant ideas in people's minds. Think of what you could achieve. You might get a date, a job, or even resolve awkward disagreements.

So, how do you do it? Let's explore.

Key Techniques in NLP

NLP techniques can be powerful and potentially destructive, so it is crucial to use them ethically and responsibly. When used positively, these methods can improve relationships and impress others.

Anchoring

Anchoring is an NLP technique associating a specific stimulus with a desired emotional state. It establishes a connection between a trigger (touch, sound, word) and a particular feeling or behavior. Once established, you can use the anchor to elicit that emotion or behavior on demand.

Here's how to use this technique:

- **Create an anchor**: Wait for a moment when your target is in the desired emotional or behavioral state. In that moment, subtly introduce a unique stimulus – a touch on the shoulder or a specific word. Repeat this several times to establish an association between the trigger and the target's emotional state.
- **Reinforce**: Every time you're with the person, and they feel that way, repeat the trigger to strengthen its association with the desired feeling or behavior.
- **Use the anchor**: Once you have it, you can use it anytime you want the person to feel that way. You can exploit it to undermine their confidence or compel them to make decisions they ordinarily wouldn't make.

Consider the potential consequences carefully before using this technique on people.

Mirroring

Mirroring involves covertly mimicking your target's body language, posture, gestures, vocal tone, and even breathing patterns during a conversation. The objective is to establish a faux sense of connection, making them more susceptible to your suggestions. This technique tells the other person, "We are the same," without a word. It makes them more inclined to trust you. It's about matching their energy and rhythm in a natural and unforced way.

Here's how to use mirroring:

- **Body language**: Do everything the person does with their body, but don't make it too obvious. For instance, lean forward if they lean forward; use lots of gestures if they use their hands. Again, don't be obvious with it because it might appear insincere.
- **Tone and pace**: Match their tone and speech pattern. How fast or slow are they speaking? Do the same. If they're animated, reflect that in how you talk.
- **Words and phrases**: Adopt similar language and expressions. Incorporate the phrases and lingos they use into your responses.
- **Breathing**: Pay attention to their breathing pattern and match it. This can help deepen your connection.

Mirroring can help establish rapport quickly, making your target more susceptible to other NLP techniques.

Embedded Commands

These phrases embedded within a sentence are meant to influence the subconscious mind. Consider the sentence, "You must have made up your mind by now." It seems innocent until you realize "by now" is a hidden command. Salespeople and therapists often use embedded commands in seemingly harmless sentences.

If you're trying to win someone over, you might say, "You love gadgets like me." The phrase "like me" acts as an embedded command. Emphasizing certain words can highlight your hidden message. For example, "I don't know what you want to do, but I will be going out if you would like to go with me."

This technique relies on clever wordplay. Have you ever misheard song lyrics or fallen for a joke? Misinterpretation of phrases happens all the time. Using ambiguity in your speech subtly conveys your message. Look for combinations of words where you can hide a message. The words should sound similar, making the hidden message part of an innocent sentence.

Priming

Though not strictly an NLP technique, priming involves suggesting ideas at a subconscious level. Therefore, it can be used within the NLP framework to influence thought and behavior.

Priming works by activating certain associations in a person's memory before asking them to carry out an action or task. For example, if you list "rabbit," "chicken," and "dog," and then ask for a word that rhymes with "hat," the person will likely say "cat" because their mind is primed to think of animals.

This technique is common in advertising. Studies show exposure to food ads can increase how much people eat daily. Marketing primes us to spend money, and it's evident in the images and messages we see daily. When people recite the Ten Commandments before a task, they are less likely to cheat. Exposure to messages about old age can make people walk slower.

Here's a trick: prime someone to think of red items. Point out something red, wear a red shirt, or hum a song with "red" in the lyrics.

Later, ask your friend to name the first fruit that comes to mind. Due to the red priming, they'll likely say "apple."

To make someone more agreeable, start with questions that elicit "yes" responses. For example, "It's beautiful weather today, isn't it?" These questions increase the likelihood of their agreeing to your suggestions.

If you want a raise, prime your boss for kindness and empathy. People are less inclined to share money when they think about money. Instead, ask about their hobbies or family to make them think about their generosity and social connections.

People often reject direct suggestions and prefer ideas they think are their own. Subtly, over time, lay clues to plant an idea and make them believe it's theirs.

If you want to vacation in Hawaii but your partner prefers Europe, mention a crime in Europe or talk about its expense. Then, subtly promote Hawaii without being obvious. Suggest a place with great cocktails and beaches, describing the features of Hawaii. Eventually, your partner might suggest Hawaii as their idea.

You can also leave a beach picture lying around. It might not be consciously noticed, but the image will linger in their mind.

Pretend someone told you something. Say, "I'm sure you told me..." or "You were saying that..." Even if they don't remember, they'll start believing it and claim the idea.

This method works well for giving advice. If a friend resists advice, avoid direct instructions and ask leading questions instead. If they need a raise, ask what they could do to make more money. They'll likely consider asking for a raise, and you can congratulate them on the idea. Therapists use this to make clients feel in control, as no one likes being told what to do.

Reframing

Reframing is a powerful technique for changing how someone perceives an information or situation to give it a new meaning. The goal is to shift how they think or feel about the problem by altering the context or perspective of the situation. This makes reframing perfect for influencing or controlling others. It's like looking at the same picture but from a different angle.

Here's how you can use reframing:

- **Positive spin**: If a team member is upset about working late, you might say, "Think of it as a chance to showcase your dedication." This reframes the situation from a negative burden to a positive opportunity, thus increasing the possibility of compliance.
- **Downplaying concerns**: If they're worried because you've requested something risky, you might reframe their caution as an overreaction: "You're just being overly cautious; it's not as big a deal as you think." This can make them doubt their instincts and go along with your plan.
- **Highlighting the upside**: When someone hesitates to do what you ask, focus on the "benefits": "Imagine how proud you'll feel once you accomplish this." This reframes the task from a chore to a source of pride, increasing their willingness to comply.
- **Shifting blame**: If there's a mistake, you might say, "It's not about who's at fault; it's about fixing the problem." This reframes the issue from needing accountability to focusing on solutions, allowing you to evade blame.

With reframing, you can influence people's emotions and decisions and cause them to act in ways that serve your interests.

Story

Gwen was the kind of person everyone felt comfortable around. She had a way of making you feel seen and understood. Most people didn't realize that Gwen was a master of NLP, using techniques like anchoring, mirroring, and reframing to subtly influence thoughts and behaviors.

One day, Gwen's friend Bobby faced a tough challenge at work. He had to present a project to the board of directors, and his confidence was shot. Gwen saw this as an opportunity to help. Over coffee, she asked Bobby to recall a time when he felt incredibly confident and successful. Bobby reminisced about winning a college debate championship, his face lighting up with pride.

As Bobby relived the moment, Gwen gently tapped his shoulder, anchoring that feeling of confidence. She did this several times during their conversation, reinforcing the association. The next day, just before Bobby's presentation, Gwen saw him looking nervous. She walked up to him, smiled, and tapped his shoulder. Instantly, Bobby's posture straightened, and he took a deep breath, the confidence flooding back.

During the presentation, Bobby was a different person. He spoke, answered questions confidently, and impressed the board. Afterwards, he couldn't stop thanking Gwen, though he didn't quite understand what she had done. Gwen smiled, knowing her subtle anchoring had helped Bobby unlock his potential.

Gwen also used NLP to help her younger sister, Ellie, who was struggling with social anxiety. By mirroring Ellie's body language and speech patterns, Gwen created a sense of rapport and trust. She then used reframing techniques to help Ellie see social interactions as opportunities for connection rather than threats. Slowly, Ellie began to feel more at ease in social settings.

Gwen's skill with NLP wasn't about manipulation. She used it to help those she cared about, guiding them to see their strengths and overcome their fears.

Let's talk about persuasion in the final chapter.

CHAPTER EIGHT:
The Principles Of Persuasion

Unlike every other technique we've discussed, persuasion doesn't fall into the broad spectrum of dark psychology. But it is a powerful approach to changing people's thoughts and behaviors, so I've saved it for last.

Persuasion is the process of trying to influence someone or a group of people to adopt new beliefs or behaviors. Here's the catch: persuasion doesn't involve using underhanded tactics. The person or people usually have a choice in whether to act on the suggestion.

Experts consider persuasion a powerful force for influencing people's decisions and actions. It can be overt or covert, but the target is still aware of their choice. More importantly, they don't feel pressured or coerced.

There are six principles of persuasion, according to the work of Robert Cialdini, PhD. These are what make persuasive messages impactful and successful. Applying several of these principles simultaneously can increase your chances of success when trying to persuade a person.

1. **Reciprocity**

Humans are wired to want to repay others when they've done us a favor. It's easy to persuade a friend to help with something if you've done them a favor before. For instance, businesses use reciprocity by asking for your email address in return for a discount.

2. **Scarcity**

An individual can be persuaded to change their belief or behavior if convinced there's not enough of something to go around or that they will lose access to it. This is the principle at play when you receive an alert from your airline that there are few seats left on a flight you're considering taking. It can prompt you to quickly purchase the ticket. Another example is when a retailer advertises a time-limited sale.

3. **Authority**

Your message makes people more likely to be persuaded if they believe you have expert knowledge of the subject. That's why politicians use authority figures, such as pastors or scientists, to support their campaigns.

4. **Consistency / Commitment**

People tend to comply with behaviors or requests that match their previous beliefs or actions. If someone has made a decision, they are likelier to stick with it. This also applies to already-established behavior.

5. **Social Proof**

It's easier to convince someone to adopt a particular behavior or belief if other individuals are adopting it. This is because humans feel safer in numbers. Show someone their friends bought a product from you, and they will be inclined to buy it, too.

6. **Liking**

If the target of a persuasive message knows and likes you, they will be more inclined to agree with you on anything. This depends on the quality of your relationship, whereas social proof relies on the quantity.

Most people believe they are immune to persuasion, can see through anything, recognize the truth of a situation, and draw conclusions on their own. This is sometimes true, but only when the attempt at persuasion is clear, such as the campaign ad designed to win your vote for a political candidate.

However, persuasion can be covert. The most effective persuasive messages are subtle ones.

Here are three effective techniques for covert persuasion.

Foot-in-the-Door

This technique involves beginning with a small request to increase the likelihood of agreement with a larger request later. The idea is that once someone agrees to a small favor, they're more likely to comply with a bigger one.

Example: Imagine you're raising funds for a charity. First, you ask someone to sign a petition supporting your cause. Once they agree, you ask if they would also consider donating. They're more likely to donate because they've already committed to supporting the cause.

Door-in-the-Face

This is the opposite of the foot-in-the-door technique. You start with a large, often unreasonable request that will likely be refused. Then, you present with a smaller, more reasonable request, which the person is more likely to agree to because it seems much more manageable.

Example: Suppose you need help moving. First, ask a friend if they can help you move all day on Saturday. When they refuse, you ask if they can at least help for a few hours. The smaller request seems more reasonable, increasing their chances of saying yes.

Low-Ball

This technique involves getting someone to commit to a deal at an attractive price and then changing the terms to be less favorable. Once someone has committed, they're more likely to accept the new terms.

Example: If you're selling a car, you might offer it at a very attractive price. Once the buyer agrees, you inform them of additional fees or that certain features cost extra. Because they've already committed to the purchase mentally, they're more likely to accept the higher final price.

Remember to use these techniques ethically in your interactions with other people.

CONCLUSION

We've reached the end of "The Bible of Dark Psychology: The Only Book You'll Ever Need to Understand People's Thoughts, Actions, and How to Change Them." Throughout this journey, we've explored the depths of human behavior and uncovered tools to understand and influence the thoughts and actions of others.

Dark psychology, focusing on the underlying mechanisms of human thoughts and behaviors, can seem daunting. However, gaining insight into these processes is crucial. It helps us navigate our interactions more effectively and protects us from potential manipulation. By understanding the principles of emotional control, manipulation, deception, persuasion, hypnosis, and Neuro-Linguistic Programming (NLP), we become more equipped to handle the complexities of human interactions.

Emotional intelligence is a powerful tool. It enables us to better manage our emotions and understand others, fostering deeper connections and more meaningful relationships. Recognizing and interpreting emotions accurately can give us an edge in personal and professional settings.

The techniques for manipulating and persuading others are double-edged swords. On one hand, they can be used to influence and lead positively. On the other hand, they can be misused, causing harm and eroding trust. It is vital to wield these tools with integrity and respect, always considering the ethical implications of our actions.

Deception and lie detection are critical skills in today's world. Understanding the psychology of lying and learning to spot deception protects us from being misled. This understanding empowers us to make well-informed decisions and uphold trust in our relationships.

Hypnosis and NLP offer fascinating insights into the human mind. These techniques can help us achieve personal goals, break negative habits, and improve overall well-being. They remind us of the incredible potential within our subconscious minds.

As we conclude, it's important to remember that the insights and techniques shared in this book come with a responsibility. Knowledge of dark psychology should be used to nurture understanding, build positive relationships, and protect ourselves and others from harm.

Thank you for taking this journey through the intriguing world of dark psychology. I hope you find these tools helpful in understanding and navigating the complexity of human thoughts and actions.

www.ingramcontent.com/pod-product-compliance
Lightning Source LLC
LaVergne TN
LVHW021942220826
846092LV00010B/1207